150
RECIPES
series
D0477704
150
CHICKEN
recipes
150
CHRISTMAS
recipes
150
CUPCAKE
& MUFFIN
recipes
150
FAST
& SIMPLE
recipes
150
GLUTEN-FREE
recipes
150
GRANDMA'S
recipes
150
HEALTHY
recipes
150
INDIAN
recipes
150
ONE-POT
recipes
150
PASTA
recipes
150
SLOW
COOKER
recipes
150
STIR-FRY
recipes
150
STUDENT
recipes
150
TAPAS
recipes
150
VEGETARIAN
recipes

150

CHRISTMAS
recipes

INSPIRED IDEAS FOR
EVERYDAY COOKING

CONTENTS

INTRODUCTION

Christmas is a time for celebrating and enjoying fabulous food and drink in the company of loved ones. It's the perfect occasion to gather family and friends together for a feast of flavours and festive treats.

Whatever your food and drink requirements for Christmas are, whether you're catering for a crowd or entertaining a smaller group, we've got it all covered in this comprehensive collection of delicious Christmas recipes. From starters, sides and sauces, to mains, desserts and drinks, we've got inspiring recipes to suit all tastes, plus we include a chapter dedicated to some truly tempting Christmas bakes and treats.

Planning ahead is key to a successful Christmas day, and the more you can do in advance the easier it will be to complete the rest of the preparations on the day. The Christmas cake and Christmas pudding, as well as mincemeat for the mince pies, can all be made a few months in advance – in fact, they will improve given this maturing time. Homemade sweets and treats can also be made ahead and carefully stored, ready for the festivities to begin. A freezer is really handy too for preparing dishes for the big day, and many sauces, soups, pies and bakes are ideal for making and freezing in advance. Compiling a countdown to Christmas, plus a time plan for the actual day will both help to avoid any last minute hitches.

So with the help of this brilliant book of sensational Christmas recipes, you can get organised and plan what you're going to cook, ensuring hassle-free festivities and a thoroughly joyful Christmas with family and friends. Cheers!

We start things off with a flavour-packed chapter of appetizing starters and mouthwatering nibbles, some of which can handily be prepared in advance. Top picks for starters include Broccoli and Stilton Soup, Gravadlax or Mixed Antipasto Meat Platter, whilst quick, easy nibbles feature tasty morsels like Honey Sesame Sausages, Stuffed Olives and Cheese Straws.

Next we concentrate on the all-important Christmas mains, be it meat, fish or vegetable-based dishes. Turkey is the traditional roast to serve on Christmas Day and we include a fantastic foolproof recipe for this, but if something else is your preference, we include a super selection of choice mains. Impress your guests with a wonderful centrepiece like Yuletide Goose, Roast Pork Loin or Festive Beef Wellington, or if fish takes your fancy, then prime picks include Poached Salmon or Roast Monkfish with Boulangère Potatoes. For those who prefer a non-meat main, try a tempting dish like Mixed Nut Roast, Asparagus and Tomato Tart or Lentil and Mushroom Pie.

Turn to the next chapter for a tasty selection of sides and sauces. We feature the ultimate recipe for Perfect Roast Potatoes, alongside other family favourites like Braised Red Cabbage, Bacon-wrapped Sausages and Cauliflower Cheese. For popular sauces, choose from Rich Onion Gravy, Cranberry Sauce or Rich Bread Sauce, not forgetting a tasty stuffing like Chestnut and Sausage Stuffing.

Our next chapter, featuring decadent desserts and drinks, includes a tempting choice of sumptuous hot and cold desserts and drinks, all ideal for feeding a crowd and sure to impress. We include prepare-ahead desserts like Boozy Chocolate Cheesecake or Peach Melba Meringue, plus traditional favourites like Festive Sherry Trifle or Rich Christmas Pudding. For no-fuss drinks and cocktails, enjoy sipping on Buck's Fizz or Kir Royale, or winter warmers like Mulled Ale, Mulled Wine and Hot Brandy Chocolate.

Finally we focus on some really scrumptious Christmas bakes and treats, perfect for when you crave a sweet treat. Children will love making Christmas bakes like Christmas Tree Biscuits and Holly Cupcakes, or indulge your guests in some delectable homemade sweets such as Espresso Truffles, Peanut Brittle and Whisky Fudge. Homemade treats like these make lovely edible gifts too, either wrapped in cellophane and tied attractively or presented in a gift basket or box.

STARTERS & NIBBLES

CHESTNUT & PANCETTA SOUP

Serves: 6 **Prep: 15 mins** **Cook: 45–50 mins**

Ingredients

- 3 tbsp olive oil
- 175 g/6 oz pancetta, cut into strips
- 2 onions, finely chopped
- 2 carrots, finely chopped
- 2 celery sticks, finely chopped
- 350 g/12 oz dried chestnuts, soaked overnight
- 2 garlic cloves, finely chopped
- 1 tbsp finely chopped fresh rosemary
- 1 litre/1¾ pints chicken stock
- salt and pepper (optional)
- 1 tbsp extra virgin olive oil, for drizzling

Method

1. Heat the olive oil in a large saucepan, add the pancetta and cook over a medium heat, stirring frequently, for 2–3 minutes, until starting to brown.
2. Add the onions, carrots and celery and cook, stirring frequently, for 10 minutes, or until light golden and soft.
3. Drain the chestnuts, add to the pan with the garlic and rosemary and stir well. Pour in the stock, bring to a simmer and cook, uncovered, for 30–35 minutes until the chestnuts are beginning to soften and break down.
4. Season to taste with salt and pepper, if using. Ladle the soup into warmed bowls, drizzle with extra virgin olive oil and serve immediately.

★ Variation

If you can't get chestnuts, replace them with 300 g/10½ oz sliced chestnut mushrooms, mixed with 15 g/½ oz dried porcini mushrooms, soaked overnight. Include the soaking water in the soup.

BROCCOLI & STILTON SOUP

Serves: 4 **Prep: 15 mins** **Cook: 35 mins**

Ingredients

- 40 g/1½ oz butter
- 2 onions, chopped
- 1 large potato, chopped
- 750 g/1 lb 10 oz broccoli florets
- 1.5 litres/2½ pints vegetable stock
- 150 g/5½ oz Stilton cheese, diced
- pinch of ground mace
- salt and pepper (optional)
- croûtons, to serve

Method

1. Melt the butter in a large saucepan. Add the onions and potato and stir well. Cover and cook over a low heat for 7 minutes. Add the broccoli and stir well, then re-cover the pan and cook for a further 5 minutes.
2. Increase the heat to medium, pour in the stock and bring to the boil. Reduce the heat, season with salt and pepper, if using, and re-cover. Simmer for 15–20 minutes, until the vegetables are tender.
3. Remove from the heat, strain into a bowl, reserving the vegetables, and leave to cool slightly. Put the vegetables into a food processor, add a ladleful of the stock and process to a smooth purée. With the motor running, gradually add the remaining stock.
4. Return the soup to the rinsed-out pan and reheat gently, but do not allow it to boil. Remove from the heat and stir in the cheese until melted and thoroughly combined. Stir in the mace and add salt and pepper, if using. Ladle into warmed bowls and serve immediately with croûtons.

CLASSIC MELON, PARMA HAM & PECORINO SALAD

Serves: 4 **Prep: 10–15 mins** **Cook: No cooking**

Ingredients

400 g/14 oz watermelon flesh, thinly sliced

400 g/14 oz honeydew melon flesh, thinly sliced

400 g/14 oz cantaloupe melon flesh, thinly sliced

140 g/5 oz sliced Parma ham

25 g/1 oz pecorino cheese shavings

25 g/1 oz fresh basil

Dressing

4 tbsp light olive oil

4 tbsp aged sherry vinegar

salt and pepper (optional)

Method

1. Arrange the watermelon, honeydew melon and canteloupe melon slices on a large serving platter. Tear any large Parma ham slices in half, then fold them all over and around the melon.
2. To make the dressing, put the oil and vinegar in a jam jar, season well with salt and pepper, if using, screw on the lid and shake well. Drizzle over the melon and Parma ham.
3. Sprinkle over the cheese shavings and basil and serve immediately.

CHICKEN LIVER PÂTÉ

Serves: 4

Prep: 20 mins, plus chilling

Cook: 10 mins

Ingredients

- 200 g/7 oz butter
- 225 g/8 oz trimmed chicken livers, thawed if frozen
- 2 tbsp Marsala
- 1½ tsp chopped fresh sage
- 1 garlic clove, roughly chopped
- 150 ml/5 fl oz double cream
- salt and pepper (optional)
- fresh sage leaves, to garnish
- Melba toast, to serve

Method

1. Melt 40 g/1½ oz of the butter in a large, heavy-based frying pan. Add the chicken livers and cook over a medium heat for 4 minutes on each side. They should be brown on the outside but still pink in the centre. Transfer to a food processor and process until finely chopped.
2. Add the Marsala to the pan and stir, scraping up any sediment with a wooden spoon, then add to the food processor with the chopped sage, garlic and 100 g/3½ oz of the remaining butter. Process until smooth. Add the cream, season to taste with salt and pepper, if using, and process until thoroughly combined and smooth. Spoon the pâté into a dish or individual ramekins, smooth the surface and leave to cool completely.
3. Melt the remaining butter in a small saucepan, then spoon it over the surface of the pâté, leaving any sediment in the pan. Top with a sage leaf. Leave to cool, then cover and chill in the refrigerator. Serve with Melba toast.

2
3

BAKED OREGANO LOBSTER

Serves: 4 **Prep: 20–25 mins** **Cook: 30 mins**

Ingredients

4 frozen lobster tails, each weighing 175 g/6 oz, thawed and patted dry

4 tbsp olive oil

1 large shallot, very finely chopped

2 garlic cloves, very finely chopped

6 tbsp fine dried breadcrumbs

2 tsp dried oregano

finely grated rind of 2 lemons

1 tbsp very finely chopped fresh flat-leaf parsley

1 tbsp olive oil, for drizzling

salt and pepper (optional)

Method

1 Preheat the oven to 180°C/350°F/Gas Mark 4. Bring a kettle of water to the boil. Select a roasting tin that will hold the lobster tails uprigh

2 Put a lobster tail on a chopping board, shell down. Use a pair of scissors to cut lengthways through the shell without cutting through the tail fan and being careful not to crush the shell Use a small knife to cut the tail meat in half lengthways without cutting through the shell.

3 Use the scissors to cut away the tough cartilag on top of the shell. Use the tip of a knife to cut out the black intestinal vein and remove. Repe with the remaining tails. Cover and refrigerate the tails until required.

4 Heat the oil in a small frying pan. Add the shall and fry for 1–2 minutes, until golden. Add the garlic and stir for a further 1 minute, or until the shallot is soft. Stir in the breadcrumbs, oregano, lemon rind and parsley and season with salt and pepper, if using.

5 Very lightly season inside the split tails with salt and pepper, if using, then place them in the roasting tin, using balls of foil to wedge them upright, if necessary. Divide the oregano mixtur between the four split tails, lightly pressing it int the splits, but not packing it in, and covering h

the tails. You might have a little left over, depending on the size of the tails. Drizzle with oil.

Add enough boiling water to the tin to come halfway up the sides of the tails, taking care not to get any water on the stuffing. Bake in the preheated oven for 20 minutes, until the flesh at the thickest part under the stuffing is white. Remove from the oven and serve immediately.

SCALLOPS WITH PEA PURÉE

Serves: 4 **Prep: 25 mins** **Cook: 12–14 mins**

Ingredients

- 500 g/1 lb 2 oz frozen peas
- 30 g/1 oz fresh mint leaves, roughly chopped
- 150 g/5½ oz butter
- 12 fat scallops, roes attached, if possible, and removed from their shells
- salt and pepper (optional)

Method

1. Bring a large saucepan of water to the boil, then add the frozen peas. Bring back to the boil and simmer for 3 minutes. Drain the peas, then put them in a food processor or blender with the mint, 100 g/3½ oz of the butter and salt, if using.
2. Process to a smooth purée, adding a little hot water if the mixture needs loosening. Cover and keep warm.
3. Pat the scallops dry, then season with salt and pepper, if using. Place a large frying pan over a high heat and add the remaining butter. When the butter starts to smoke, add the scallops and sear them for 1–2 minutes on each side. They should be brown and crisp on the outside but light and moist in the middle. Remove the pan from the heat.
4. Spread a spoonful of pea purée on each of four plates and place three scallops on top of each. Serve immediately.

DEVILLED CRAB RAMEKINS

Serves: 4 **Prep: 10 mins** **Cook: 25 mins**

Ingredients

- g/¼ oz melted butter, for greasing
- 175 g/6 oz crabmeat
- 1 large egg, beaten
- 4 tbsp crème fraîche
- juice of 1 lime
- 1 tsp hot chilli sauce
- 85 g/3 oz fresh white breadcrumbs
- 4 tbsp freshly grated Parmesan cheese
- tsp paprika, for sprinkling
- t and pepper (optional)

To serve

- lime wedges
- salad leaves
- asted wholemeal bread

Method

1. Preheat the oven to 200°C/400°F/Gas Mark 6. Brush four 150-ml/5-fl oz ramekins with butter and place on a baking sheet.
2. Mix the crabmeat with the egg, crème fraîche, lime juice and chilli sauce. Stir in the breadcrumbs and season with salt and pepper, if using.
3. Spoon the mixture into the prepared ramekins and sprinkle with the cheese. Bake in the preheated oven for about 15 minutes, until golden and bubbling.
4. Sprinkle with the paprika and serve hot with lime wedges, salad leaves and toasted wholemeal bread.

FESTIVE PRAWN COCKTAIL

Serves: 8 **Prep: 25 mins** **Cook: No cooking**

Ingredients

125 ml/4 fl oz tomato ketchup

1 tsp chilli sauce

1 tsp Worcestershire sauce

2 ruby grapefruits

8 lettuce leaves, shredded

1 kg/2 lb 4 oz cooked tiger prawns, peeled and deveined

2 avocados, peeled, stoned and diced

lime slices and fresh dill sprigs, to garnish

Mayonnaise

2 large egg yolks

1 tsp English mustard powder

1 tsp salt

pinch of pepper

300 ml/10 fl oz groundnut oil

1 tsp white wine vinegar

Method

1 To make the mayonnaise, put the egg yolks in a bowl, add the mustard powder, salt and pepper and beat together well. Begin whisking the egg yolks, adding the oil just one drop at a time, making sure that this has been thoroughly absorbed before adding another drop and whisking well.

2 Continue adding the oil one drop at a time until the mixture thickens and stiffens – at this point, whisk in the vinegar, then continue to dribble in the remaining oil very slowly in a thin stream, whisking constantly, until you have used up all the oil and have a thick mayonnaise.

3 Mix the mayonnaise, tomato ketchup, chilli sauce and Worcestershire sauce together in a small bowl. Cover with clingfilm and refrigerate.

4 Cut off a slice from the top and bottom of each grapefruit, then peel off the skin and all the white pith. Cut between the membranes to separate the segments.

5 When ready to serve, make a bed of shredded lettuce in the bases of eight glass dishes. Divide the prawns, grapefruit segments and avocados between them and spoon over the mayonnaise dressing. Serve the cocktails garnished with lime slices and dill sprigs.

3
4

GRAVADLAX

Serves: 10

Prep: 15 mins, plus chilling

Cook: No cooking

Ingredients

2 salmon fillets, with skin on, each weighing 450 g/1 lb

6 tbsp roughly chopped fresh dill

115 g/4 oz sea salt

50 g/1¾ oz sugar

1 tbsp roughly crushed white peppercorns

12 thin slices of brown bread, buttered and lemon wedges, to serve

Method

1. Rinse the salmon fillets under cold running wate and dry with kitchen paper. Put one fillet skin side down in a non-metallic dish.
2. Mix the dill, salt, sugar and peppercorns together in a small bowl. Spread this mixture over the fillet in the dish and put the second fille skin side up on top. Put a plate the same size as the fish on top and weigh down with three o four food cans.
3. Chill in the refrigerator for 2 days, turning the fish about every 12 hours and basting with any juices that come out of the fish.
4. Remove the salmon from the brine and thinly slice, without slicing the skin, as you would smoked salmon. Cut the buttered bread into triangles and serve with the salmon and lemon wedges.

2
2

MUSHROOMS ON RYE TOAST

Serves: 4 **Prep: 15 mins** **Cook: 10 mins**

Ingredients

- 3 tbsp olive oil
- 2 large garlic cloves, crushed
- 225 g/8 oz chestnut mushrooms, sliced
- 225 g/8 oz wild mushrooms, sliced
- 2 tsp lemon juice
- 2 tbsp finely chopped fresh flat-leaf parsley
- 4 slices of rye bread
- sea salt and pepper (optional)

Method

1. Heat the oil in a large frying pan over a medium–low heat. Add the garlic and cook for a few seconds.
2. Increase the heat to high. Add the chestnut mushrooms to the pan and cook, stirring constantly, for 3 minutes. Add the wild mushrooms and cook for a further 2 minutes.
3. Stir in the lemon juice and parsley and season with salt and pepper, if using.
4. Lightly toast the rye bread, then transfer to a serving plate. Spoon the mushroom mixture ove the toast and serve immediately.

ROASTED PEPPER & GARLIC FOCACCIA

Serves: 6

Prep: 30 mins, plus rising

Cook: 45 mins

Ingredients

- 1 tbsp olive oil, for oiling
- 500 g/1 lb 2 oz strong white flour
- 1½ tsp salt
- 1 sachet easy-blend dried yeast
- 350 ml/12 fl oz lukewarm water
- 4 tbsp olive oil
- 10 g/¼ oz strong white flour, for dusting
- 1 red pepper, halved and deseeded
- 3 garlic cloves

Method

1. Preheat the oven to 240°C/475°F/Gas Mark 9. Oil a baking sheet. Put the flour and salt into a mixing bowl and stir in the yeast. Add the water and 3 tablespoons of the oil and mix to a soft dough.
2. Turn out the dough onto a lightly floured surface and knead until smooth. Return to the bowl, cover and leave to rest in a warm place for 30 minutes.
3. Meanwhile, place the red pepper cut-side down on a baking sheet, add the unpeeled garlic cloves and roast in the preheated oven for 20 minutes, until the skins are charred. Remove from the oven (do not switch off the oven), peel the pepper and cut it into strips, then squeeze the flesh from the garlic and chop.
4. Turn out the dough onto a lightly floured surface and lightly knead until smooth. Roll out to a rectangle and press into the prepared sheet with your knuckles. Scatter over the red peppers and garlic, pressing them into the dough. Cover and leave to rise in a warm place for about 1 hour, until doubled in size.
5. Drizzle the remaining oil over the dough and bake for 20–25 minutes, until golden brown and firm. Turn out and leave to cool on a wire rack.

3
5

LEEK & GOAT'S CHEESE TARTLETS

Serves: 6 **Prep: 15 mins** **Cook: 20 mins**

Ingredients

375 g/13 oz ready-rolled puff pastry (1 rectangular sheet, 35 x 23 cm/14 x 9 inches)

40 g/1½ oz butter

350 g/12 oz baby leeks, thickly sliced diagonally

1 tbsp chopped fresh oregano

125 g/4½ oz goat's cheese, sliced or crumbled

1 tbsp milk, for brushing

salt and pepper (optional)

Method

1 Preheat the oven to 220°C/425°F/Gas Mark 7. Cut the pastry into six 12-cm/4½-inch squares.

2 Place the pastry squares on a baking sheet and use the tip of a sharp knife to score each one about 1 cm/½ inch from the edge all around.

3 Melt the butter in a frying pan, add the leeks and gently fry, stirring frequently, for 4–5 minutes, until soft. Add the oregano, season with salt and pepper, if using, and divide the leek mixture between the pastry squares, placing it inside the scored lines.

4 Top each tartlet with cheese and brush the pastry with the milk. Bake in the preheated oven for 12–15 minutes, until risen and golden brown. Serve warm.

BAKED FIGS WITH GORGONZOLA

Serves: 4 **Prep: 15 mins** **Cook: 10 mins**

Ingredients

1 mixed-grain demi baguette, cut into 8 x 2-cm/¾-inch thick slices (total weight 100 g/3½ oz)

8 small fresh figs

55 g/2 oz Gorgonzola cheese, rind removed, cut into 8 squares

p clear wildflower honey

Method

1 Preheat the oven to 180°C/350°F/Gas Mark 4. Lightly toast the bread on both sides, then transfer to a small baking sheet.

2 Cut a cross in the top of each fig, lightly press a cube of cheese into each one, then place a fig on top of each slice of toast. Bake in the preheated oven for 5–6 minutes, until the figs are hot and the cheese is just melting.

3 Transfer to a plate or chopping board. Drizzle with honey and serve immediately.

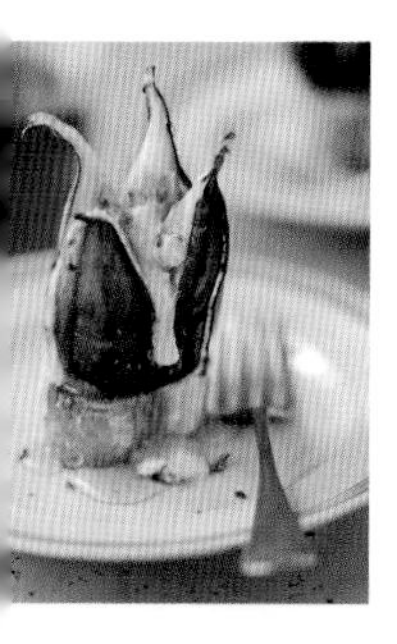

GARLIC-STUFFED MUSHROOMS

Serves: 4 **Prep: 15 mins** **Cook: 10–12 mins**

Ingredients

4 large field mushrooms
4 sprays olive oil
2–3 garlic cloves, crushed
2 shallots, roughly chopped
25 g/1 oz fresh wholemeal breadcrumbs
8 fresh basil sprigs
25 g/1 oz ready-to-eat dried apricots, chopped
1 tbsp pine nuts
55 g/2 oz feta cheese
pepper (optional)
fresh basil sprigs, to garnish

Method

1 Preheat the oven to 180°C/350°F/Gas Mark 4. Remove the stalks from the mushrooms and set aside. Spray the bases of the mushroom caps with the oil and place cap-side down in a roasting tin.

2 Put the mushroom stalks in a food processor with the garlic, shallots and breadcrumbs and process briefly. Add the basil sprigs in the food processor with the apricots, pine nuts and cheese. Add pepper to taste, if using.

3 Process for 1–2 minutes until the mixture has a stuffing consistency, then divide between the mushroom caps.

4 Bake in the preheated oven for 10–12 minutes, or until the mushrooms are tender and the stuffing is crisp on the top. Serve garnished with basil sprigs.

BLUE CHEESE & HERB PÂTÉ

Serves: 4

Prep: 15 mins,
plus chilling

Cook: 1 min

Ingredients

150 g/5½ oz low-fat soft cheese
350 g/12 oz fromage frais
115 g/4 oz blue cheese, crumbled
g/2 oz dried cranberries, finely chopped
bsp chopped fresh herbs, uch as parsley, chives, dill and tarragon
85 g/3 oz butter
2 tbsp chopped walnuts
4 slices granary toast, to serve

Method

1 Beat the soft cheese to soften, then gradually beat in the fromage frais until smooth. Add the blue cheese, cranberries and herbs. Stir together. Spoon the mixture into four 150-ml/5-fl oz ramekins or small dishes and carefully smooth the tops.

2 Clarify the butter by gently heating it in a small saucepan until melted. Skim any foam off the surface and discard. Carefully pour the clear yellow top layer into a small jug, leaving the milky liquid in the pan. The yellow layer is the clarified butter. Discard the liquid left in the pan.

3 Pour a little of the clarified butter over the top of each pâté and sprinkle with the walnuts. Chill in the refrigerator for at least 30 minutes until firm. Serve with granary toast.

FILO-WRAPPED ASPARAGUS WITH PARMESAN

Serves: 6 **Prep: 30 mins** **Cook: 14–16 mins**

Ingredients

1–2 tsp salt

18 plump asparagus spears, tough ends snapped off

10 g/¼ oz butter, for greasing

3 sheets filo pastry, each measuring 45 x 24 cm/ 17¾ x 9½ inches

125 g/4½ oz butter, melted

90 g/3¼ oz freshly grated Parmesan cheese

salt (optional)

Dip

150 ml/5 fl oz good-quality mayonnaise

150 ml/5 fl oz natural yogurt

10–12 fresh basil leaves, torn into small pieces

1 garlic clove, crushed

Method

1 Add 1–2 teaspoons of salt to a saucepan of water, bring to the boil, add the asparagus and blanch for 30–40 seconds, then transfer to a bowl of cold water using a slotted spoon. Drain and pat dry with kitchen paper.

2 Preheat the oven to 200°C/400°F/Gas Mark 6. Lightly grease a baking tray. Lay one sheet of the pastry on a work surface, covering the remaining sheets with a damp tea towel to prevent them drying out. Brush the pastry with a little of the melted butter and sprinkle with one third of the cheese, then cut into six 15 x 12-cm/6 x 4½-inch rectangles.

3 Place an asparagus spear at one end of each rectangle and roll up. Transfer to the prepared tray. Repeat with the remaining pastry, cheese and asparagus. Brush with the remaining butter and bake in the preheated oven for 12–14 minutes, until crisp and golden brown.

4 To make the dip, mix the mayonnaise, yogurt, basil and garlic together in a small bowl. Serve the filo-wrapped asparagus warm or cold with the dip.

GARLIC & MOZZARELLA CRACK BREAD

Serves: 4

Prep: 15 mins, plus standing

Cook: 25 mins

Ingredients

1 loaf ciabatta bread

125 ml/4 fl oz olive oil

4 garlic cloves, finely chopped

2 spring onions, finely chopped

pinch of salt

100 g/3½ oz mozzarella cheese

Method

1. Preheat the oven to 200°C/400°F/Gas Mark 6.
2. Line a baking tray with enough foil to enclose the bread, shiny side up. Set aside.
3. Use a serrated knife to cut the bread into 2.5-cm/1-inch diamond shapes, without cuttin all the way through, and set aside. It is importa to keep the loaf in one piece.
4. Mix the oil, garlic, spring onions and salt together. Gently prise open the cracks in the bread and generously brush with the oil mixtur
5. Shred the mozzarella cheese. Use your fingers to divide the mozzarella cheese between the cracks. Wrap the bread in the foil, pushing the cracks back together so that the bread is as compact as possible.
6. Bake in the preheated oven for 15 minutes. Uncover the bread and return it to the oven for a further 10 minutes until the cheese has melte and the top is golden and crisp.
7. Leave to stand for 2–3 minutes, then serve.

4
5

HONEY SESAME SAUSAGES

Makes: 24 **Prep: 10 mins** **Cook: 20–25 mins**

Ingredients

1 tbsp olive oil, for oiling
2 tbsp clear honey
1 tbsp olive oil
24 lean cocktail sausages
2 tbsp sesame seeds

Method

1. Preheat the oven to 190°C/375°F/Gas Mark 5. Brush a non-stick baking sheet with a little oil and place in the oven to heat.
2. Meanwhile, whisk together the honey and oil in a large bowl, add the sausages and toss wel to coat.
3. Spread the sesame seeds on a large piece of greaseproof paper and roll each sausage in th seeds until well coated.
4. Remove the baking sheet from the oven and place the sausages on it. Bake the sausages in the preheated oven for 10 minutes. Turn the sausages over and bake for a further 10–15 minutes, until well browned and sticky.
5. Serve warm or cold.

MINI TURKEY PIES WITH CRANBERRY RELISH

Serves: 12

Prep: 20 mins, plus cooling

Cook: 33–35 mins

Ingredients

300 g/10½ oz ready-made shortcrust pastry, chilled

10 g/¼ oz plain flour, for dusting

1 egg yolk mixed with 1 tbsp water, for glazing

300 g/10½ oz minced turkey

4 spring onions, finely chopped

2 garlic cloves, finely chopped

leaves from 4 fresh thyme sprigs

1 tsp ground allspice

2 egg yolks

salt and cayenne pepper (optional)

Cranberry relish

1 tbsp olive oil

1 red onion, thinly sliced

85 g/3 oz frozen cranberries

3 tbsp cranberry sauce

4 tbsp ruby port or red wine

Method

1. Preheat the oven to 180°C/350°F/Gas Mark 4. Line a 12-hole muffin tin with squares of non-stick baking paper.
2. Thinly roll out the pastry on a lightly floured surface. Use a 12.5-cm/5-inch plain round cutter to stamp out 12 rounds. Press these gently into the prepared tin, so the pastry stands just above the top of the tin in soft pleats. Brush the top edges with a little of the egg glaze.
3. Put the turkey, onions, garlic and thyme leaves into a mixing bowl. Sprinkle over the allspice and a little salt and cayenne pepper, if using, then stir in the egg yolks until well mixed. Spoon the filling into the pie cases and press the tops flat with the back of a teaspoon.
4. Bake in the preheated oven for 30 minutes, or until the pastry is golden and the filling is cooked through. Leave to cool in the tins for 5 minutes, then loosen with a round-bladed knife and transfer to a wire rack until needed.
5. Meanwhile, to make the relish, heat the oil in a frying pan, add the onion and cook until just beginning to soften. Add the remaining ingredients and cook for 3–4 minutes, or until the cranberries are soft. Spoon over the top of the baked pies and serve.

MIXED ANTIPASTO MEAT PLATTER

Serves: 4 **Prep: 20 mins** **Cook: No cooking**

Ingredients

1 cantaloupe melon

55 g/2 oz Italian salami, thinly sliced

8 slices prosciutto

8 slices bresaola

8 slices mortadella

4 plum tomatoes, thinly sliced

4 fresh figs, halved

115 g/4 oz black olives, stoned

2 tbsp shredded fresh basil leaves

4 tbsp olive oil

pepper (optional)

1 tbsp extra virgin olive oil, for drizzling

Method

1. Cut the melon in half, scoop out and discard the seeds, then cut the flesh into 8 wedges. Arrange the wedges on one half of a large serving platter.
2. Arrange the salami, prosciutto, bresaola and mortadella in loose folds on the other half of the platter. Arrange the tomato slices and fig halves on the platter.
3. Scatter the olives over the antipasto. Sprinkle the basil over the tomatoes and drizzle with the olive oil. Season to taste with pepper, if using, then drizzle with extra virgin olive oil and serve immediately.

BLINIS WITH PRAWNS & WASABI CREAM

Serves: 6

Prep: 30 mins, plus chilling & standing

Cook: 10–15 mins

Ingredients

- 350 g/12 oz plain flour
- 125 g/4½ oz buckwheat flour
- 2 tsp easy-blend dried yeast
- 600 ml/1 pint milk, warmed
- 6 eggs, separated
- 3 tbsp unsalted butter, melted
- 5 tbsp soured cream
- 50 g/1¾ oz clarified butter

Wasabi cream

- 200 ml/7 fl oz soured cream or crème fraîche
- ½ tsp wasabi paste, or to taste
- salt (optional)

To serve

- 300 g/10½ oz cooked prawns, peeled and deveined
- 50 g/1¾ oz pickled ginger, thinly sliced
- 2 tbsp fresh coriander leaves

Method

1. Sift together the plain flour and buckwheat flour into a large bowl and stir in the yeast. Make a hollow in the centre and add the milk, then gradually beat in the flour until you have a smooth batter. Cover the batter and chill in the refrigerator overnight.
2. Two hours before you need the blinis, remove the batter from the refrigerator and leave to stand for 1 hour 20 minutes to bring back to room temperature.
3. Beat in the egg yolks, melted butter and soured cream. In a separate bowl, whisk the egg whites until they hold stiff peaks, then gradually fold into the batter. Cover and leave to rest for 30 minutes.
4. Meanwhile, make the wasabi cream. Mix the soured cream and wasabi paste together in a small bowl until combined. Taste and add a little more wasabi paste if you like it hotter. Season to taste with salt, if using, then cover and chill.
5. To cook the blinis, heat a little of the clarified butter in a non-stick frying pan over a medium-high heat. When hot and sizzling, drop in 3–4 tablespoons of the batter, spaced well apart, and cook until puffed up and tiny bubbles appear around the edges.

- Flip them over and cook for a few more minutes on the other side. Remove from the pan and keep warm while you cook the remaining batter.
- To serve, spoon a little of the wasabi cream onto a blini, add 1–2 prawns and a few slices of pickled ginger, then scatter with a few coriander leaves.

DEVILS & ANGELS ON HORSEBACK

Makes: 32 **Prep: 30 mins** **Cook: 10–15 mins**

Ingredients

Devils

8 rindless lean bacon rashers

8 canned anchovy fillets in oil, drained

16 whole blanched almonds

16 ready-to-eat prunes

Angels

8 rindless lean bacon rashers

16 smoked oysters, drained if canned

8 fresh thyme sprigs, to garnish

Method

1 Preheat the oven to 200°C/400°F/Gas Mark 6. To make the devils, cut each bacon rasher in half lengthways and gently stretch with the back of a knife. Cut each anchovy fillet in half lengthways. Wrap half an anchovy around each almond and press them into the cavity where the stones have been removed from the prunes. Wrap a strip of bacon around each prune and secure with a cocktail stick.

2 To make the angels, cut each bacon rasher in half lengthways and gently stretch with the back of a knife. Wrap a bacon strip around each oyster and secure with a cocktail stick.

3 Place the devils and angels on a baking sheet and bake in the preheated oven for 10–15 minutes, until sizzling hot and the bacon is cooked. Garnish with the thyme and serve hot.

STUFFED OLIVES

Serves: 6 **Prep: 20 mins** **Cook: No cooking**

Ingredients

4 tbsp Spanish extra virgin olive oil

1 tbsp sherry vinegar, or to taste

2 tbsp very finely chopped fresh parsley

finely grated rind of ½ orange

18 large stoned black olives

18 large stoned green olives

12 anchovy fillets in oil, drained

½ grilled red pepper in oil, drained and cut into 12 small pieces

12 blanched almonds

Method

1 Whisk together the oil, vinegar, parsley and orange rind in a small serving bowl, adding extra vinegar to taste. Set aside until needed.

2 Make a lengthways slit in 12 of the black olives and 12 of the green olives without cutting all th way through.

3 Roll up the anchovy fillets and gently press ther into the cavities of 6 of the slit green olives and of the slit black olives.

4 Use the pieces of red pepper to stuff the remaining slit olives. Slip a blanched almond into the centre of each of the remaining olives.

5 Add all the olives to the bowl of dressing and stir gently. Serve with wooden cocktail sticks for spearing the olives.

MOZZARELLA CROSTINI WITH PESTO & CAVIAR

Serves: 4 **Prep: 25 mins** **Cook: 15 mins**

Ingredients

8 slices white bread, crusts removed

3 tbsp olive oil

0 g/7 oz firm mozzarella cheese, diced

6 tbsp lumpfish roe

Pesto

75 g/2¾ oz fresh basil, finely chopped

35 g/1¼ oz pine nuts, finely chopped

2 garlic cloves, finely chopped

3 tbsp olive oil

Method

1. Preheat the oven to 180°C/350°F/Gas Mark 4. Using a sharp knife, cut the bread into fancy shapes, such as half-moons, stars and Christmas trees. Drizzle with the oil, transfer to an ovenproof dish and bake in the preheated oven for 15 minutes.
2. While the bread is baking, make the pesto. Put the basil, pine nuts and garlic in a small bowl. Pour in the oil and stir well to combine.
3. Remove the bread shapes from the oven and leave to cool. Spread a layer of pesto on all of the shapes, top each one with a piece of mozzarella cheese and some lumpfish roe and serve immediately.

CHEESE STRAWS

Makes: 24

Prep: 15 mins, plus chilling

Cook: 10–15 mins

Ingredients

- 115 g/4 oz plain flour, plus extra for dusting
- pinch of salt
- 1 tsp curry powder
- 55 g/2 oz butter, plus extra for greasing
- 55 g/2 oz grated Cheddar cheese
- 1 egg, beaten
- poppy seeds and cumin seeds, for sprinkling

Method

1. Sift the flour, salt and curry powder into a bowl. Add the butter and rub in until the mixture resembles breadcrumbs. Add the cheese and half the egg and mix to a dough. Wrap in clingfilm and chill in the refrigerator for 30 minutes.
2. Preheat the oven to 200°C/400°F/Gas Mark 6, and grease several baking trays. On a floured work surface, roll out the dough to 5 mm/¼ inch thick. Cut into 7.5 x 1-cm/3 x ½-inch strips. Pinch the strips lightly along the sides and place on the prepared baking trays.
3. Brush the strips with the remaining egg and sprinkle half with poppy seeds and half with cumin seeds. Bake in the preheated oven for 10–15 minutes, or until golden. Transfer to wire racks to cool.

BROAD BEAN & MINT HUMMUS WITH CRUDITÉS

Serves: 4 **Prep: 25 mins** **Cook: 10 mins**

Ingredients

350 g/12 oz podded broad beans

2 tbsp virgin olive oil

1 tsp cumin seeds, crushed

3 spring onions, thinly sliced

2 garlic cloves, finely chopped

25 g/1 oz fresh mint, torn into pieces

25 g/1 oz fresh flat-leaf parsley, finely chopped

juice of 1 lemon

60 g/2¼ oz Greek-style natural yogurt

sea salt and pepper (optional)

To serve

1 red pepper, deseeded and cut into strips

1 yellow pepper, deseeded and cut into strips

4 celery sticks, cut into strips

½ cucumber, halved, deseeded and cut into strips

Method

1 Half-fill the base of a steamer with water, bring to the boil, then put the beans in the top of the steamer, cover with a lid and steam for 10 minutes, or until tender.

2 Meanwhile, heat the oil in a frying pan over a medium heat. Add the cumin, spring onions ar garlic and cook for 2 minutes, or until the onior is soft.

3 Put the beans in a food processor or blender, add the onion mixture, herbs, lemon juice and yogurt and season with a little salt and peppe if using. Process to a coarse purée, then spoon into a dish set on a large plate.

4 Arrange the vegetable strips around the hummus and serve.

STUFFED PEPPER POPPERS WITH CHEESE & CHICKEN

Makes: 12 **Prep: 30–35 mins** **Cook: 15 mins**

Ingredients

- 1 tbsp olive oil, for oiling
- 70 g/2½ oz full-fat cream cheese
- 2 garlic cloves, finely chopped
- 2 tsp finely chopped fresh rosemary
- 1 tbsp finely chopped fresh basil
- 1 tbsp finely chopped fresh parsley
- 15 g/½ oz freshly grated Parmesan cheese
- 150 g/5½ oz cooked chicken breast, finely chopped
- 3 spring onions, finely chopped
- 12 mixed coloured baby peppers, about 350 g/12 oz total weight
- sea salt and pepper (optional)

Method

1. Preheat the oven to 190°C/375°F/Gas Mark 5. Lightly brush a large baking sheet with oil.
2. Put the cream cheese, garlic, rosemary, basil and parsley in a bowl, then add the Parmesan cheese and stir with a metal spoon.
3. Mix in the chicken and spring onions, then season with a little salt and pepper, if using.
4. Slit each pepper from the tip up to the stalk, leaving the stalk in place, then make a small cu just to the side, so that you can get a teaspoon into the centre to scoop out the seeds.
5. Fill each pepper with some of the chicken mixture, then place on the prepared baking sheet. Cook in the preheated oven for 15 minutes, or until the peppers are soft and light brown in patches.
6. Leave to cool slightly on the baking sheet, then transfer to a serving plate. Serve warm or cold. These are best eaten on the day they are made and should be kept in the refrigerator if serving cold.

BRUSCHETTA WITH BROAD BEANS & GOAT'S CHEESE

Serves: 6 **Prep: 30 mins** **Cook: 25 mins**

Ingredients

- 600 g/1 lb 5 oz shelled small broad beans (about 2.5 kg/5 lb 8 oz unshelled weight)
- 3 tbsp extra virgin olive oil
- 1 tbsp lemon juice
- 1 tbsp chopped fresh mint leaves
- 6 slices ciabatta
- 1 large garlic clove, halved
- 1 tsp extra virgin olive oil, for drizzling
- 6 tbsp soft fresh goat's cheese
- sea salt flakes and pepper (optional)

Method

1. Bring a large saucepan of water to the boil. Add the beans, bring back to the boil and coo for 3 minutes, until just tender. Rinse under cold running water and drain. Slip off the bean skins and discard.
2. Toss the beans with the oil, lemon juice and most of the mint. Season with a little salt and pepper, if using.
3. Tip the bean mixture into a food processor anc process briefly to a chunky purée.
4. Toast the bread on both sides. While the bread still warm, rub one side of each slice with the c garlic clove. Drizzle with oil.
5. Cut each bread slice in half. Spread with the bean mixture, top with goat's cheese and serv immediately.

★ Variation

Feta cheese makes a delicious alternative to th goat's cheese. As it's very salty, however, don't add any salt to the beans.

MAINS

TRADITIONAL ROAST TURKEY

Serves: 4

Prep: 25 mins

Cook: 3 hours 15 mins, plus standing

Ingredients

1 oven-ready turkey, weighing 5 kg/11 lb
1 garlic clove, finely chopped
100 ml/3½ fl oz red wine
75 g/2¾ oz butter
seasonal vegetables, to serve

Stuffing

100 g/3½ oz button mushrooms, chopped
1 onion, chopped
1 garlic clove, chopped
85 g/3 oz butter
100 g/3½ oz fresh breadcrumbs
2 tbsp finely chopped fresh sage
1 tbsp lemon juice
salt and pepper (optional)

Port & cranberry sauce

100 g/3½ oz sugar
275 ml/9 fl oz port
175 g/6 oz fresh cranberries

Method

1 Preheat the oven to 200°C/400°F/Gas Mark 6.

2 To make the stuffing, put the mushrooms in a saucepan with the onion, garlic and butter and cook for 3 minutes.

3 Remove from the heat and stir in the remaining stuffing ingredients. Fill the neck end of the turkey with the stuffing and truss with string.

4 Put the turkey in a roasting tin. Rub the garlic over the bird and pour the wine over. Add the butter and roast in the preheated oven for 30 minutes. Baste, then reduce the temperature to 180°C/350°F/Gas Mark 4 and roast for a further 40 minutes.

5 Baste again and cover with foil. Roast for a further 2 hours, basting regularly. Check that the bird is cooked by inserting a knife between the legs and body. If the juices run clear, it is cooked.

6 Remove from the oven, loosely cover with foil and leave to stand for 25 minutes.

7 Meanwhile, to make the sauce, put the sugar, port and cranberries in a saucepan. Heat over a medium heat until almost boiling. Serve the turkey with seasonal vegetables and the port and cranberry sauce.

★ **Variation**

If you prefer a rich stuffing, try adding some sausage meat. Simply replace half the mushrooms with 50 g/1¾ oz good-quality sausage meat and add to the pan with the mushrooms, onion and garlic in Step 2. You could also replace all the mushrooms with 100 g/3½ oz dried chestnuts, soaked overnight, drained and roughly chopped.

TRADITIONAL ROAST CHICKEN

Serves: 6

Prep: 20 mins, plus resting

Cook: 1 hour 45 mins

Ingredients

1 x 2.25-kg/5-lb free-range chicken

55 g/2 oz butter

2 tbsp chopped fresh lemon thyme

1 lemon, quartered

125 ml/4 fl oz white wine

salt and pepper (optional)

fresh thyme sprigs, to garnish

Method

1. Preheat the oven to 220°C/425°F/Gas Mark 7. Make sure the chicken is clean, wiping it inside and out with kitchen paper, and place in a roasting tin. Put the butter into a bowl and soften with a fork, then mix in the chopped thyme and season with salt and pepper, if using. Butter the chicken all over with the herb butter, inside and out, and place the lemon quarters inside the body cavity. Pour the wine over the chicken.
2. Roast in the centre of the preheated oven for 20 minutes. Reduce the oven temperature to 190°C/375°F/Gas Mark 5 and roast for a further 1¼ hours, basting frequently. Cover with foil if the skin begins to brown too much. If the tin dries out, add a little more wine or water.
3. The chicken is cooked if the juices run clear when the thickest part of the leg is pierced with a sharp knife or skewer. Remove from the oven and transfer to a warmed serving plate, loosely cover with foil and leave to rest for 10 minutes before carving. Place the roasting tin on the hob and gently bubble the pan juices over a low heat until they have reduced and are thick and glossy. Season with salt and pepper, if using. Serve the chicken with the pan juices, garnished with thyme sprigs.

CHICKEN ROULADES

Serves: 6

Prep: 40 mins, plus chilling

Cook: 1 hour 5 mins– 1 hour 10 mins

Ingredients

6 skinless, boneless chicken breasts, each weighing 175 g/6 oz

200 g/7 oz fresh chicken mince

1 tbsp olive oil

2 shallots, roughly chopped

1 garlic clove, crushed

150 ml/5 fl oz double cream

3 fresh sage leaves, chopped

1 tbsp chopped fresh parsley

1 tbsp brandy

1 tbsp vegetable oil

18 pancetta rashers

2 tsp plain flour

200 ml/7 fl oz white wine

200 ml/7 fl oz chicken stock

salt and pepper (optional)

Method

1. Place each chicken breast between two sheet of clingfilm and flatten with a rolling pin as evenly as possible. Trim neatly and chill until needed.
2. Meanwhile, chop the chicken trimmings and m with the mince in a bowl. Heat the olive oil in a frying pan over a medium heat, add the shallo and garlic and cook for 5 minutes.
3. Add to the mince with the cream, herbs and brandy and mix well together. Season with salt and pepper, if using, cover and chill in the refrigerator for 15 minutes.
4. Divide the mince mixture between the breasts, spreading it to within 1 cm/½ inch of the edge and then roll each breast up and wrap secure in foil.
5. Poach in a large saucepan of simmering wate for 20 minutes, remove with a slotted spoon an leave to cool completely.
6. Preheat the oven to 190°C/375°F/Gas Mark 5. Put the vegetable oil into a roasting tin and pu in the oven to heat.

Meanwhile, remove the foil and tightly wrap each roulade in 3 pancetta rashers. Roll the roulades in the hot oil, then roast in the oven for 25–30 minutes, turning twice, until they are brown and crisp.

Remove the roulades and keep warm. Place the tin on the hob, add the flour and stir well until a smooth paste forms. Gradually whisk in the wine and stock. Simmer for 4–5 minutes, then season with salt and pepper, if using. Slice the roulades and serve with the gravy.

DUCK WITH MADEIRA & BLUEBERRY SAUCE

Serves: 4

Prep: 20 minutes, plus marinating

Cook: 25 mins, plus standing

Ingredients

4 duck breasts, with skin on

4 garlic cloves, chopped

grated rind and juice of 1 orange

1 tbsp chopped fresh parsley

salt and pepper (optional)

Madeira & blueberry sauce

150 g/5½ oz blueberries

275 ml/9 fl oz Madeira

1 tbsp redcurrant jelly

Method

1. Use a sharp knife to make several shallow diagonal cuts in each duck breast. Put the duc into a glass bowl with the garlic, orange juice and rind, and the parsley. Season with salt and pepper, if using, and stir well. Turn the duck in th mixture until thoroughly coated. Cover the bow with clingfilm and leave in the refrigerator to marinate for at least 1 hour.
2. Heat a dry, non-stick frying pan over a medium heat. Add the duck breasts and cook for 4 minutes, then turn them over and cook for a further 4 minutes, or to taste. Remove from the heat, cover and leave to stand for 5 minutes.
3. To make the sauce, halfway through the cooking time, put the blueberries, Madeira anc redcurrant jelly into a separate saucepan. Brin to the boil. Reduce the heat and simmer for 10 minutes, then remove from the heat.
4. Slice the duck breasts, transfer to warmed plat and serve with the sauce poured over.

ROAST DUCK WITH APPLE WEDGES

Serves: 4 **Prep: 30 mins** **Cook: 1 hour**

Ingredients

- 4 duckling portions, about 350 g/12 oz each
- 4 tbsp dark soy sauce
- 2 tbsp light muscovado sugar
- 2 red-skinned apples
- 2 green-skinned apples
- juice of 1 lemon
- 2 tbsp clear honey
- a few bay leaves
- salt and pepper (optional)
- freshly cooked vegetables, to serve

Apricot sauce

- 400 g/14 oz canned apricots in fruit juice
- 4 tbsp sweet sherry

Method

1. Preheat the oven to 190°C/375°F/Gas Mark 5. Trim any excess fat from the duck. Place on a wire rack over a roasting tin and prick all over with a fork or a clean, sharp needle.
2. Brush the duck with the soy sauce. Sprinkle over the sugar and season with pepper, if using. Cook in the preheated oven, basting occasionally, for 50 minutes–1 hour, or until the meat is cooked through and the juices run cle when a skewer is inserted into the thickest par of the meat.
3. Meanwhile, core the apples and cut each int 6 wedges, then place in a small bowl and mix with the lemon juice and honey. Transfer to a small roasting tin, add a few bay leaves and season to taste with salt and pepper, if using. Cook in the oven alongside the duck for 20–2 minutes until tender. Discard the bay leaves.
4. To make the sauce, place the apricots in a blender or food processor with the can juices and the sherry. Process until smooth.
5. Just before serving, heat the apricot sauce in small saucepan. Serve the duck with the app wedges, apricot sauce and vegetables.

YULETIDE GOOSE

Serves: 4–6

Prep: 15 mins

**Cook: 2 hours 45 mins–
3 hours 15 mins**

Ingredients

1 x 3.5–4.5-kg/7¾–10-lb oven-ready goose

1 tsp salt

4 pears

1 tbsp lemon juice

55 g/2 oz butter

2 tbsp clear honey

Method

1 Preheat the oven to 220°C/425°F/Gas Mark 7. Use a fork to prick the skin of the goose all ove then rub with the salt. Place the bird upside down on a rack in a roasting tin. Roast in the preheated oven for 30 minutes. Drain off the fat. Turn the bird over and roast for a further 15 minutes, then drain again.

2 Reduce the oven temperature to 180°C/350°F/ Gas Mark 4 and roast the goose for 15 minute per 450 g/1 lb. Cover with foil 15 minutes befor the end of the cooking time. The bird is cooke if the juices run clear when a knife is inserted between the legs and body. Remove from the oven and transfer to a warmed serving platter, loosely cover with foil and leave to rest.

3 Meanwhile, peel and halve the pears, then brush with the lemon juice. Melt the butter an honey in a saucepan over a low heat, then ac the pears. Cook, stirring, for 5–10 minutes until tender. Remove from the heat, arrange the pe around the goose and pour the sweet juices over the bird, then serve.

ROAST PHEASANT

Serves: 4

Prep: 40 mins, plus resting

Cook: 1 hour 10 mins

Ingredients

100 g/3½ oz butter, slightly softened

1 tbsp chopped fresh thyme

1 tbsp chopped fresh parsley

2 oven-ready young pheasants

4 tbsp vegetable oil

125 ml/4 fl oz red wine

and pepper (optional)

Game chips

650 g/1 lb 7oz potatoes

ower oil, for deep-frying

Method

1 Preheat the oven to 190°C/375°F/Gas Mark 5. Put the butter in a small bowl and mix in the thyme and parsley. Lift the skins off the pheasants, taking care not to tear them, and push the herb butter under the skins. Season to taste with salt and pepper, if using.

2 Pour the oil into a roasting tin, add the pheasants and roast in the preheated oven for 45 minutes, basting occasionally. Remove from the oven, pour over the wine, then return to the oven and cook for a further 15 minutes, or until cooked through. The birds are cooked if the juices run clear when a knife is inserted between the legs and body.

3 To make the game chips, peel the potatoes, cut into wafer-thin slices and place in a bowl of cold water. Heat enough oil for deep-frying in a large saucepan or a deep fryer to 180–190°C/350–375°F, or until a cube of bread browns in 30 seconds. Drain the potato slices and pat dry with kitchen paper. Deep-fry, in batches, for 2–3 minutes, stirring to prevent sticking, then remove with a slotted spoon. Drain on kitchen paper.

4 Remove the birds from the oven, loosely cover with foil and leave to rest for 15 minutes. Serve on a warmed serving platter with the chips.

ROAST PORK LOIN

Serves: 6

Prep: 25 mins, plus resting

Cook: 2 hours 10 mins

Ingredients

1.8 kg/4 lb flat piece pork loin, backbone removed and rind scored

2½ tsp salt

¼ tsp pepper

3 garlic cloves, crushed

2 tbsp chopped fresh rosemary

4 fresh rosemary sprigs

225 ml/8 fl oz dry white wine

fresh rosemary sprigs, to garnish

cooked seasonal vegetables, to serve

Method

1 Preheat the oven to 230°C/450°F/Gas Mark 8. Put the pork on a work surface, skin-side down. Make small slits in the meat all over the surface Season with ½ teaspoon of the salt and the pepper. Rub the garlic all over the meat surfac and sprinkle with the chopped rosemary.

2 Roll up the loin and secure the rosemary sprigs on the outside with fine string. Make sure that the joint is securely tied. Season the rind with th remaining salt to give a good crackling.

3 Transfer the meat to a roasting tin and roast in the preheated oven for 20 minutes, or until the fat has started to run. Reduce the oven temperature to 190°C/375°F/Gas Mark 5 and pour over half the wine. Roast for a further 1 hc 40 minutes, basting meat occasionally with the pan juices.

4 Remove from the oven and leave to rest in a warm place for 15 minutes. Remove the string and the rosemary, then carve into thick slices.

5 Pour off all but 1 tablespoon of the fat from the tin. Add the remaining wine to the pan juices and bring to the boil, scraping up and stirring in any sediment from the base. Spoon over the meat and serve immediately with vegetables, garnished with extra sprigs of rosemary.

GLAZED GAMMON

Serves: 8 **Prep: 20 mins** **Cook: 4 hours 20 mins**

Ingredients

4 kg/9 lb gammon
1 apple, cored and chopped
1 onion, chopped
300 ml/10 fl oz cider
6 black peppercorns
1 bouquet garni
1 bay leaf
50 cloves
4 tbsp demerara sugar

Method

1. Put the gammon into a large saucepan and add enough cold water to cover. Bring to the boil and skim off any foam that rises to the surface. Reduce the heat and simmer for 30 minutes.
2. Drain the gammon and return to the pan. Add the apple, onion, cider, peppercorns, bouquet garni, bay leaf and a few of the cloves. Pour in fresh water to cover and bring back to the boil. Cover and simmer for 3 hours 20 minutes.
3. Preheat the oven to 200°C/400°F/Gas Mark 6. Remove the pan from the heat and set aside to cool slightly. Remove the gammon from the cooking liquid and, while it is still warm, loosen the rind with a sharp knife, peel off and discard.
4. Score the fat into diamond shapes and stud with the remaining cloves. Place the gammon on a rack in a roasting tin and sprinkle with the sugar. Roast in the preheated oven, basting occasionally with the cooking liquid, for 20 minutes. Serve hot or cold.

PRIME RIB OF BEEF AU JUS

Serves: 8

Prep: 10 mins, plus standing

Cook: 1 hour 40 mins–2 hours 25 mins

Ingredients

2.7 kg/6 lb rib of beef
55 g/2 oz butter, softened
1½ tsp sea salt flakes
1 tbsp pepper
2 tbsp flour
1 litre/1¾ pints beef stock
freshly cooked vegetables and roast potatoes, to serve

Method

1. Place the beef bone-side down in a deep-sided roasting tin. Rub the entire surface of the meat with butter, and coat evenly with the salt and pepper.
2. Leave the beef to reach room temperature for 1 hour. Preheat the oven to 230°C/450°F/Gas Mark 8. Place the beef in the preheated oven and roast, uncovered, for 20 minutes to sear the outside of the meat.
3. Reduce the oven temperature to 160°C/325°F/Gas Mark 3 and roast for 15 minutes per 450 g/1 lb of meat for medium rare (plus or minus 15 minutes for well-done and rare respectively). Transfer to a large platter and cover with foil. Leave to rest for 30 minutes before serving.
4. Meanwhile, pour off all but 2 tablespoons of the fat from the tin and place the tin over a medium heat. Add the flour and simmer, stirring with a wooden spoon, for 1 minute, or until a thick paste forms.
5. Pour in a ladleful of stock and bring to the boil, then beat into the paste, scraping all the caramelized drippings from the base of the tin until smooth. Repeat with the remaining stock, a ladleful at a time.

Simmer for 10 minutes until reduced and slightly thickened. Strain the sauce and keep warm.

Cut the beef free from the bone and carve thinly. Serve the jus alongside the carved beef, accompanied by vegetables and roast potatoes.

FESTIVE BEEF WELLINGTON

Serves: 4 **Prep: 30 mins** **Cook: 1 hour 10 mins**

Ingredients

750 g/1 lb 10 oz thick beef fillet

25 g/1 oz butter

2 tbsp vegetable oil

1 garlic clove, chopped

1 onion, chopped

175 g/6 oz chestnut mushrooms, thinly sliced

1 tbsp chopped fresh sage

350 g/12 oz ready-made puff pastry, thawed if frozen

1 egg, beaten

salt and pepper (optional)

Method

1 Preheat the oven to 220°C/425°F/Gas Mark 7. Put the beef in a roasting tin, spread with the butter and season to taste with salt and pepper, if using. Roast in the preheated oven for 30 minutes, then remove from the oven. Do not switch off the oven.

2 Meanwhile, heat the oil in a saucepan over a medium heat. Add the garlic and onion and cook, stirring, for 3 minutes. Stir in salt and pepper to taste, if using, the mushrooms and the sage and cook, stirring frequently, for 5 minutes. Remove from the heat.

3 Roll out the pastry into a rectangle large enough to enclose the beef, then place the beef in the centre and spread the mushroom mixture over it. Bring the long sides of the pastry together over the beef and seal with beaten egg. Tuck the short ends over, trimming away the excess pastry, and seal. Place on a baking sheet seam-side down and make two slits in the top. Decorate with pastry shapes made from the trimmings and brush with the beaten egg. Bake for 40 minutes. Remove from the oven, cut into thick slices and serve.

2
3

STEAK WITH PANCAKES & MUSTARD SAUCE

Serves: 6 **Prep: 20 mins** **Cook: 10–15 mins**

Ingredients

- 6 fillet steaks, about 150 g/5½ oz each
- 1 tbsp olive oil
- 1 tsp unsalted butter
- 200 ml/7 fl oz crème fraîche
- 2 tsp wholegrain mustard
- salt and pepper (optional)
- 2 tbsp snipped fresh chives, to garnish

Pancakes

- 400 g/14 oz potatoes
- 55 g/2 oz self-raising flour
- ½ tsp baking powder
- 200 ml/7 fl oz milk
- 2 eggs, beaten
- vegetable oil, for frying

Method

1. To make the pancakes, cook the potatoes in their skins in a large saucepan of boiling water until tender. Drain and leave until cool enough to handle. Peel, then pass through a potato rice or mash and press through a sieve, into a bowl.
2. Sift the flour and baking powder over the potatoes, then add a little of the milk and mix well. Add the remaining milk and the eggs and beat well to make a smooth batter.
3. Heat a little vegetable oil in a 20-cm/8-inch non-stick frying pan over a medium heat. Add a ladleful of the batter to cover the base of the pan and cook until little bubbles appear on the surface. Turn over and cook for a further 1 minute, or until nicely browned, then turn out and keep warm. Repeat until you have cooked 6 pancakes.
4. Season the steaks to taste with salt and pepper if using. Heat the oil and butter in a non-stick frying pan over a high heat until sizzling. Add th steaks and cook to your liking, then remove fror the pan and keep warm. Add the crème fraîch and mustard to the pan, stir and heat through. Season well with salt and pepper, if using. Serve each steak with a folded pancake and some sauce, scattered with a few snipped chives.

LAMB WITH ROQUEFORT & WALNUT BUTTER

Serves: 4 **Prep: 15 mins, plus chilling** **Cook: 10 mins**

Ingredients

- 55 g/2 oz butter
- 140 g/5 oz Roquefort cheese, crumbled
- 2 tbsp finely chopped walnuts
- 8 lamb noisettes
- salt and pepper (optional)
- snipped chives, to garnish (optional)
- freshly cooked vegetables, to serve

Method

1. Cream half the butter in a bowl with a wooden spoon. Beat in the cheese and walnuts until thoroughly combined and season to taste with salt and pepper, if using. Turn out the flavoured butter onto a sheet of greaseproof paper and shape into a cylinder. Wrap and leave to chill in the refrigerator until firm.
2. Heat a ridged griddle pan, add the remaining butter and, as soon as it has melted, add the lamb noisettes and cook for 4–5 minutes on each side.
3. Transfer the lamb to warmed serving plates and top each noisette with a slice of Roquefort and walnut butter. Garnish with snipped chives, if using, and serve immediately with freshly cooked vegetables.

SMOKED SALMON RISOTTO

Serves: 4 **Prep: 20 mins** **Cook: 15–20 mins**

Ingredients

50 g/1¾ oz unsalted butter

1 onion, finely chopped

½ small fennel bulb, very finely chopped

500 g/1 lb 2 oz arborio or carnaroli rice

300 ml/10 fl oz white wine

1.2 litres/2 pints hot fish stock

150 g/5½ oz hot smoked salmon flakes

150 g/5½ oz smoked salmon slices

2 tbsp chopped fresh chervil leaves or chopped fresh flat-leaf parsley

salt and pepper (optional)

Method

1 Melt half the butter in a large saucepan over a medium heat, add the onion and fennel and cook, stirring frequently, for 5–8 minutes, until transparent and soft. Add the rice and stir well coat the grains in the butter. Cook, stirring, for 3 minutes, then add the wine, stir and simmer un most of the liquid has been absorbed.

2 With the stock simmering in a separate saucepan, add 1 ladleful to the rice and stir we Cook, stirring constantly, until nearly all the liqui has been absorbed before adding another ladleful of stock. Continue to add the remainin stock in the same way until the rice is cooked but still firm to the bite and most or all of the stock has been added.

3 Remove from the heat and stir in the two types of salmon and the remaining butter. Season wi salt and pepper, if using, and serve scattered with the chervil.

POACHED SALMON

ɪerves: 6 **Prep: 20 mins** **Cook: 6–8 mins, plus standing**

Ingredients

ɿole salmon (head on), ɔbout 2.7–3.6 kg/6–8 lb prepared weight

3 tbsp salt

3 bay leaves

10 black peppercorns

1 onion, sliced

1 lemon, sliced

ɩemon wedges, to serve

Method

1 Wipe the salmon thoroughly inside and out with kitchen paper, then use the back of a cook's knife to remove any scales that might still be on the skin. Remove the fins with a pair of scissors and trim the tail. Some people prefer to cut off the head but it is traditionally served with it on.

2 Place the salmon on the two-handled rack that comes with a fish kettle, then place it in the kettle. Fill the kettle with enough cold water to cover the salmon adequately. Sprinkle over the salt, bay leaves and peppercorns and scatter in the onion and lemon slices.

3 Place the kettle over a low heat, over two burners, and very slowly bring just to the boil.

4 Cover and simmer very gently for 6–8 minutes, then leave to stand in the hot water for 15 minutes before removing. Serve with lemon wedges for squeezing over.

GRILLED MONKFISH WITH HERB POLENTA SLICES

Serves: 4 **Prep: 10 mins** **Cook: 12–15 mins**

Ingredients

- 1 tbsp olive oil, for oiling
- 1 litre/1¾ pints boiling water
- 200 g/7 oz medium-grain polenta
- 25 g/1 oz butter
- 2 tbsp finely chopped fresh parsley
- 2 tsp chopped fresh dill
- 4 pieces monkfish fillet
- 1 tbsp olive oil
- salt and pepper (optional)
- 4 lemon wedges, to serve

Method

1. Lightly oil a rectangular baking dish or tin. Pour the water into a large saucepan, bring to the boil and stir in the polenta. Cook over a mediu heat, stirring, for 5 minutes, or until thickened ar starting to come away from the side of the par
2. Remove from the heat and stir in the butter, parsley, dill and salt and pepper, if using. Spreo evenly in the prepared dish and leave to cool. Chill in the refrigerator until set.
3. Preheat the grill or a griddle pan to high. Brush the monkfish with the oil and sprinkle with salt and pepper, if using. Arrange on the grill rack and cook for 6–8 minutes, turning once, until cooked through.
4. Meanwhile, turn out the polenta and cut into slices. Add to the grill about halfway through the fish cooking time and cook until golden, turning once.
5. Slice the monkfish and arrange on the polentc slices. Serve hot, with the lemon wedges for squeezing over.

SEAFOOD PIE WITH STILTON

Serves: 6

Prep: 30 mins, plus cooling

Cook: 30–35 mins

Ingredients

- 300 ml/10 fl oz vegetable stock
- 100 ml/3½ fl oz dry vermouth
- 3 tbsp cornflour, blended with 3 tbsp cold water
- 30 g/1 oz butter, cut into small pieces
- 6 tbsp crème fraîche
- 375 g/13 oz skinless cod fillet, cut into chunks
- 375 g/13 oz skinless salmon fillet, cut into chunks
- 225 g/8 oz raw king prawns, peeled and deveined
- 175 g/6 oz fine asparagus spears, tough ends snapped off, cut into 2.5-cm/1-inch pieces
- 115 g/4 oz Stilton cheese, crumbled
- 4 tbsp snipped fresh chives
- 500 g/1 lb 2 oz ready-made puff pastry
- plain flour, for dusting
- pepper (optional)

Method

1. Pour the stock and vermouth into a saucepan and bring to the boil. Whisk in the cornflour paste and simmer for 1 minute to make a thick sauce. Remove from the heat and stir in the butter and crème fraîche, then cover the surfac with baking paper. Leave to cool.
2. Preheat the oven to 220°C/425°F/Gas Mark 7. Stir the fish, prawns, asparagus, cheese and chives into the sauce. Season to taste with pepper, if using, then spoon into a 1.5-litre/ 2½-pint pie dish.
3. Roll out the pastry on a lightly floured surface tc a thickness of about 3 mm/⅛ inch. Cut a long 2-cm/¾-inch strip and press around the rim of the pie dish, fixing it in place with a little water. Use the remaining pastry to cover the pie. Cut the trimmings into shapes to decorate and fix them in place with a little water. Make a small hole in the centre to allow steam to escape.
4. Bake in the preheated oven for 20 minutes, unti the pastry is well risen and golden brown, then reduce the temperate to 180°C/350°F/Gas Mark 4 and bake for a further 35 minutes. Serve immediately.

ROAST MONKFISH WITH BOULANGÈRE POTATOES

Serves: 4 **Prep: 30 mins** **Cook: 40–50 mins**

Ingredients

- 40 g/1½ oz butter, melted
- 700 g/1 lb 9 oz floury potatoes very thinly sliced
- 1 onion, very thinly sliced
- 1 tbsp roughly chopped fresh thyme
- about 200 ml/7 fl oz vegetable stock
- 4 skinless monkfish fillets, about 200 g/7 oz each
- 4 tbsp olive oil
- finely pared zest of 1 lemon
- 8 tbsp chopped fresh flat-leaf parsley
- 1 garlic clove, crushed
- salt and pepper (optional)
- mixed rocket, watercress and baby spinach leaves, to serve

Method

1. Preheat the oven to 200°C/400°F/Gas Mark 6. Brush a shallow ovenproof dish with a little of the melted butter. Layer the potatoes, onion and thyme in the dish, seasoning well with salt and pepper between the layers, if using, and finishing with a layer of potatoes.
2. Pour in enough stock to come halfway up the potatoes and drizzle the remaining melted butter over the top. Bake in the centre of the preheated oven for 40–50 minutes, pressing the potatoes into the stock once or twice with a spatula until tender and browned on top.
3. Meanwhile, season the monkfish well with salt and pepper, if using. Mix together the oil, lemon zest, parsley and garlic and rub all over the fillets. Sear in a smoking hot frying pan or on a griddle pan for 1 minute on each side, or until browned. Transfer the fillets to a roasting tin, spaced well apart, and roast on the top shelf of the oven for the final 12–15 minutes of the cooking time for the potatoes, until just cooked through. Serve immediately with the potatoes and mixed salad leaves.

TURBOT STEAKS WITH PARSLEY, LEMON & GARLIC

Serves: 4 **Prep: 10 mins** **Cook: 20 mins**

Ingredients

2 tbsp olive oil, for brushing

4 turbot steaks

finely grated and juice rind of 1 lemon

2 garlic cloves, finely chopped

4 tbsp finely chopped fresh flat-leaf parsley

40 g/1½ oz toasted pine nuts

salt and pepper (optional)

freshly cooked vegetables, to serve

Method

1 Preheat the oven to 220°C/425°F/Gas Mark 7. Brush a wide, ovenproof dish with oil.

2 Place the turbot steaks in the dish, brush with c season with salt and pepper, if using, and pou over the lemon juice.

3 Mix the lemon rind, garlic, parsley and pine nu together and spoon over the fish. Drizzle with th remaining oil.

4 Bake in the preheated oven for 15–20 minutes, until the fish flakes easily with a fork. Transfer to warmed plates and serve immediately with freshly cooked vegetables.

Serves: 4 **Prep: 15 mins** **Cook: 35 mins**

Ingredients

- 10 g/¼ oz butter, for greasing
- 25 g/1 oz butter
- 2 garlic cloves, chopped
- 1 large onion, chopped
- 50 g/1¾ oz pine nuts, toasted
- 75 g/2¾ oz hazelnuts, toasted
- 50 g/1¾ oz ground walnuts
- 50 g/1¾ oz ground cashew nuts
- 100 g/3½ oz wholemeal breadcrumbs
- 1 egg, lightly beaten
- 2 tbsp chopped fresh thyme
- 275 ml/9 fl oz vegetable stock
- salt and pepper (optional)
- fresh thyme sprigs, to garnish

Cranberry & red wine sauce

- 175 g/6 oz fresh cranberries
- 100 g/3½ oz caster sugar
- 300 ml/10 fl oz red wine
- 1 cinnamon stick

Method

1. Preheat the oven to 180°C/350°F/Gas Mark 4. Grease a 450-g/1-lb loaf tin and line it with greaseproof paper.
2. Melt the butter in a saucepan over a medium heat. Add the garlic and onion and cook, stirring, for about 3 minutes. Remove the pan from the heat.
3. Grind the pine nuts and hazelnuts in a mortar with a pestle. Stir into the pan with the walnuts and cashew nuts and add the breadcrumbs, egg, thyme, stock and salt and pepper, if using.
4. Spoon the mixture into the prepared tin and level the surface. Cook in the centre of the preheated oven for 30 minutes, or until cooked through and golden and a skewer inserted into the centre of the loaf comes out clean.
5. Halfway through the cooking time, make the sauce. Put the cranberries, sugar, wine and cinnamon into a saucepan over a medium heat and bring to the boil. Reduce the heat and simmer, stirring occasionally, for 15 minutes.
6. Remove the nut roast from the oven and turn out onto a serving platter. Garnish with thyme sprigs and serve with the sauce.

4
5

VEGETABLE WELLINGTON

Serves: 6

Prep: 40 mins, **plus cooling**

Cook: 1 hour 10 mins, plus standing

Ingredients

- 4 tsp salt
- ½ tsp saffron threads
- 200 g/7 oz long-grain rice
- 250 g/9 oz onions, thinly sliced
- 3 tbsp sunflower oil
- 45 g/1½ oz soft light brown sugar
- 500 g/1 lb 2 oz butternut squash, deseeded and cut into 1-cm/½-inch pieces
- 2 tsp chilli-flavoured olive oil
- 40 g/1½ oz butter
- 2 tsp olive oil
- 3 shallots, thinly sliced
- 4 garlic cloves, finely chopped
- 600 g/1 lb 5 oz mixed mushrooms, trimmed and finely chopped
- 2 x 225 g/8 oz rolled puff pastry sheets
- 3 tbsp snipped fresh chives
- 125 g/4½ oz soft goat's cheese
- 1 egg, beaten

Method

1. Preheat the oven to 200°C/400°F/Gas Mark 6. Bring a large saucepan of water to the boil wit 3 teaspoons of the salt and the saffron. Add th rice and boil for 10–12 minutes, or until tender. Drain well and leave to cool completely.
2. Meanwhile, toss the onions with the sunflower oil and sugar. Spread the onion mixture in a shallow roasting tin. Toss the butternut squash with the chilli-flavoured oil and ½ teaspoon of the salt. Place in another shallow roasting tin. Roast the onion and squash in the preheated oven for 20–25 minutes, stirring frequently, until the onions are caramelized and the squash is tender. Leave both to cool completely.
3. Melt the butter with the olive oil in a large fryin pan over a medium heat. Add the shallots and garlic and fry for 3–5 minutes. Stir in the mushrooms with the remaining salt, increase th heat to high and fry for 12–15 minutes. Leave t cool completely.
4. Line a baking sheet with greaseproof paper. C one sheet of pastry into a 28 x 18-cm/11 x 7-in rectangle. Spread half the rice over it, leaving 1-cm/½-inch border.
5. Toss the squash, mushrooms and onions together, then stir in the chives and small piec

of the cheese. Spread across the pastry and top with the remaining rice. Brush the edge of the pastry with the beaten egg.

Lay the remaining pastry over the rice and press it onto the border. Trim away the excess and press the edges together with a fork. Glaze the surface with beaten egg. Cut 4 slashes in the top. Bake in the preheated oven, for 20–25 minutes, until golden brown. Leave to stand for 10 minutes, then serve.

ROAST BUTTERNUT SQUASH

Serves: 4 **Prep: 40 mins** **Cook: 1 hour 10 mins**

Ingredients

1 butternut squash, weighing 450 g/1 lb

1 onion, chopped

2–3 garlic cloves, crushed

4 small tomatoes, chopped

85 g/3 oz chestnut mushrooms, chopped

85 g/3 oz canned butter beans, drained, rinsed and roughly chopped

1 courgette, weighing 115 g/4 oz, grated

1 tbsp chopped fresh oregano

2 tbsp tomato purée

300 ml/10 fl oz water

4 spring onions, chopped

1 tbsp Worcestershire sauce

1 tbsp chopped fresh oregano, for sprinkling

pepper (optional)

Method

1 Preheat the oven to 190°C/375°F/Gas Mark 5. Prick the squash all over with a fork or metal skewer, then roast in the preheated oven for 40 minutes, or until tender. Remove from the oven and leave to rest until cool enough to handle.

2 Cut the squash in half, scoop out and discard the seeds, then scoop out some of the flesh, making hollows in both halves. Chop the scooped-out flesh and put it into a bowl. Place the two squash halves side by side in a large roasting tin.

3 Add the onion, garlic, tomatoes and mushroon to the squash flesh in the bowl. Add the beans, courgette, oregano and a little pepper, if using and mix well together. Spoon the filling into the two halves of the squash, packing it down as firmly as possible.

4 Mix the tomato purée with the water, spring onions and Worcestershire sauce in a small bo and pour around the squash.

5 Loosely cover with a large sheet of foil and bak for 30 minutes, or until piping hot. Serve in bowl sprinkled with chopped oregano.

3
4

WILD MUSHROOM RISOTTO

Serves: 6

Prep: 20 mins, plus soaking

Cook: 15–20 mins

Ingredients

55 g/2 oz dried ceps

4 tbsp olive oil

500 g/1 lb mixed fresh wild mushrooms, halved if large, trimmed

3–4 garlic cloves, finely chopped

55 g/2 oz butter

1 onion, finely chopped

350 g/12 oz risotto rice

50 ml/2 fl oz dry white vermouth

1.2 litres/2 pints simmering chicken or vegetable stock

115 g/4 oz freshly grated Parmesan cheese

4 tbsp chopped fresh flat-leaf parsley

salt and pepper (optional)

Method

1 Place the ceps in a heatproof bowl and add boiling water to cover. Set aside to soak for 30 minutes, then carefully lift out and pat dry. Strain the soaking liquid through a sieve lined with kitchen paper and set aside.

2 Heat 3 tablespoons of the oil in a large frying pan. Add the fresh mushrooms and stir-fry for 1–2 minutes. Add the garlic and the soaked mushrooms and cook, stirring frequently, for 2 minutes. Transfer to a plate.

3 Heat the remaining oil and half the butter in a large, heavy-based saucepan. Add the onion and cook over a medium heat, stirring occasionally, for 2 minutes, until soft.

4 Reduce the heat, stir in the rice and cook, stirring constantly, for 2–3 minutes, until the grains are translucent. Add the vermouth and cook, stirring constantly, for 1 minute, until reduced.

5 Gradually add the stock, a ladleful at a time, until all the liquid is absorbed and the rice is creamy. Add half the reserved mushroom soaking liquid and stir in the mushrooms. Season with salt and pepper, if using, and add more mushroom liquid, if necessary. Remove from the heat, stir in the remaining butter, the cheese and parsley and serve.

ASPARAGUS & TOMATO TART

erves: 4 **Prep: 35 mins** **Cook: 1 hour 10 mins**

Ingredients

butter, for greasing

75 g/13 oz ready-made ortcrust pastry, thawed if frozen

1 bunch thin asparagus spears

1–2 tsp salt

g/9 oz spinach leaves

3 large eggs, beaten

150 ml/5 fl oz double cream

1 garlic clove, crushed

10 small cherry tomatoes, halved

handful fresh basil, chopped

5 g/1 oz freshly grated Parmesan cheese

and pepper (optional)

Method

1. Preheat the oven to 190°C/375°F/Gas Mark 5. Grease a 30-cm/12-inch tart tin, then roll out the pastry and use to line the tin.
2. Cut off any excess pastry and prick the base with a fork. Cover with a piece of greaseproof paper and fill with baking beans. Bake in the preheated oven for 20–30 minutes until lightly browned. Remove from the oven and take out the greaseproof paper and beans. Reduce the oven temperature to 180°C/350°F/Gas Mark 4.
3. Meanwhile, bend the asparagus spears until they snap, and discard the woody bases. Add 1–2 teaspoons of salt to a large saucepan of water and bring to the boil. Add the asparagus and blanch for 1 minute, then remove and drain. Add the spinach to the boiling water, then remove immediately and drain very well.
4. Mix the eggs, cream and garlic together and season with salt and pepper, if using. Lay the spinach on the pastry base. Add the asparagus and tomatoes, cut side up. Scatter over the basil, then pour the egg mixture on top.
5. Transfer to the oven and bake for about 35 minutes, or until the filling has set. Sprinkle the cheese on top and leave to cool to room temperature before serving.

ROAST BEETROOT PARCELS WITH POLENTA

Serves: 4

Prep: 20 mins, plus cooling

Cook: 2 hours

Ingredients

2 tbsp olive oil, for greasing and tossing

8 small beetroots, peeled and halved

4 fresh thyme sprigs

4 tbsp grated fresh horseradish, or grated horseradish from a jar

125 g/4½ oz unsalted butter

salt and pepper (optional)

rocket leaves, to serve

Polenta

900 ml/1½ pints water

175 g/6 oz quick-cook polenta

1 tsp salt

Method

1. To make the polenta, bring the water to the bo in a large saucepan. Slowly add the polenta and salt, stirring constantly. Simmer, stirring frequently, for 30–40 minutes, until the mixture comes away from the side of the pan.
2. Grease a small roasting tin. Tip the polenta intc the tin, level the surface and leave to cool.
3. Preheat the oven to 190°C/375°F/Gas Mark 5. Toss the beetroots with enough oil to coat.
4. Place 4 beetroot halves and a thyme sprig on a square of thick foil. Season with salt and pepper, if using. Wrap in a loose parcel, sealing the edges. Repeat with the remaining beetroo halves, to make four parcels in total. Roast in th preheated oven for 1 hour, or until just tender.
5. Meanwhile, mash the horseradish with the butter, and a little salt and pepper, if using. Rol into a log using a piece of clingfilm and chill.
6. Preheat the grill to high. Slice the polenta into four rectangles. Spread out in a grill pan, brush with oil and cook under the grill for 5 minutes. Turn and grill for a further 3 minutes until crisp.
7. Arrange the polenta on serving plates. Place th beetroot and a slice of horseradish butter on t and serve with rocket.

LENTIL & MUSHROOM PIE

Serves: 6 **Prep: 30–40 mins** **Cook: 45 mins–1 hour**

Ingredients

3 tbsp olive oil

1 fennel bulb, trimmed and thinly sliced

1 carrot, diced

1 celery stick, diced

1 shallot, chopped

6 garlic cloves, chopped

500 g/1 lb 2 oz chestnut mushrooms, thickly sliced

¼ tsp salt

275 ml/9 fl oz vegetable stock

800 g/1 lb 12 oz canned green lentils, drained and rinsed

400 g/14 oz canned chopped tomatoes

2 tsp dried thyme

1 tsp light brown sugar

¼ tsp pepper

4 tbsp finely chopped fresh parsley

Potato topping

1¼ tsp salt

300 g/10½ oz sweet potatoes, chopped

600 g/1 lb 5 oz floury potatoes, thickly chopped

30 g/1 oz butter, melted

Method

1 Preheat the oven to 200°C/400°F/Gas Mark 6.

2 Heat the oil in a saucepan over a medium heat. Add the fennel, carrot, celery and shallot, and fry, stirring occasionally, for 8–10 minutes until soft. Add the garlic, mushrooms and salt and continue stirring for 5–8 minutes until the mushrooms are tender and have re-absorbed any liquid.

3 Stir the stock, lentils, tomatoes, thyme, sugar and pepper into the pan. Bring to the boil and boil for 5–8 minutes, or until the liquid has evaporated. Stir in the parsley.

4 Meanwhile, make the potato topping. Add the salt to a saucepan of water and bring to the boil. Add the sweet potatoes and boil for 5 minutes. Add the white potatoes and boil for a further 10 minutes, or until tender. Drain well and return to the pan over a low heat to steam dry. Use a potato masher or wooden spoon to beat the potatoes.

5 Spoon the filling into a 30-cm/12-inch oval pie dish, or 1.7-litre/3-pint ovenproof serving dish. Spoon the potatoes over the filling, smooth the surface and run a fork over it. Drizzle the butter over the potatoes.

Bake in the preheated oven for 20–25 minutes until the filling is bubbling. Place under a preheated grill for 3–5 minutes if you want the topping to brown. Serve immediately.

AUBERGINES STUFFED WITH BULGAR WHEAT

Serves: 4 **Prep: 35 mins** **Cook: 50 mins**

Ingredients

1 tsp each ground cumin, ground coriander, paprika, dried chilli flakes

2 tbsp olive oil

2 aubergines, cut in half lengthways

1 red onion, roughly chopped

2 garlic cloves, chopped

150 g/5½ oz fine bulgar wheat

200 ml/7 fl oz vegetable stock

3 tbsp roughly chopped fresh coriander

3 tbsp roughly chopped fresh mint

125 g/4½ oz feta cheese, crumbled

30 g/1 oz flaked almonds, toasted

1½ tbsp lemon juice

2 tsp pomegranate molasses

salt and pepper (optional)

To garnish

1 tbsp chopped fresh mint

1 tsp pomegranate molasses

125 g/4½ oz Greek-style natural yogurt

4 tbsp pomegranate seeds

Method

1 Preheat the oven to 180°C/350°F/Gas Mark 4. Mix the cumin, coriander, paprika, chilli flakes and 1½ tablespoons of the oil in a small bowl. Use a sharp knife to slice the aubergine flesh in a diagonal, criss-cross pattern, being careful not to pierce the skin. Drizzle the spice mixture over the aubergines and allow it to sink into the crosses. Place the aubergine halves on a baking sheet and roast in the preheated oven for 35 minutes until tender.

2 Meanwhile, heat the remaining oil in a large frying pan over a medium heat. Add the onion and garlic and fry for about 3–4 minutes, or until softened. Reduce the heat, add the bulgar wheat and stir well. Reduce the heat to low, pour in the stock and continue to stir until the liquid has been absorbed. Remove this mixture from the pan and transfer to a large bowl.

3 Remove the aubergines from the oven and leave to rest for 10 minutes, or until cool enough to handle. Leave the oven on. Using a dessertspoon, scoop out the centre of each aubergine half, leaving a clear edge to support the filling.

Add the aubergine flesh to the bulgar mixture. Stir in the fresh coriander, mint, cheese, almonds, lemon juice and pomegranate molasses. Stir well and season with salt and pepper, if using.

Divide the stuffing between the aubergines and return to the oven for 15 minutes. Serve immediately, garnished with the fresh mint, molasses, yogurt and pomegranate seeds.

LAYERED CASSEROLE

Serves: 4 **Prep: 20 mins** **Cook: 1 hour**

Ingredients

3 tbsp olive oil

600 g/1 lb 5 oz parsnips, thinly sliced

1 tsp fresh thyme leaves

1 tsp caster sugar

300 ml/10 fl oz double cream

600 g/1 lb 5 oz tomatoes, thinly sliced

1 tsp dried oregano

150 g/5½ oz Cheddar cheese, grated

salt and pepper (optional)

Method

1 Preheat the oven to 180°C/350°F/Gas Mark 4.

2 Heat the oil in a frying pan over a medium heat, add the parsnips, thyme, sugar and salt and pepper to taste, if using, and cook, stirring frequently, for 6–8 minutes until golden and soft

3 Spread half the parsnips over the base of a gratin dish. Pour over half the cream, then arrange half the tomatoes in an even layer across the parsnips. Season to taste with salt and pepper, if using, and scatter over half the oregano. Sprinkle over half the cheese. Top with the remaining parsnips and tomatoes. Sprinkle with the remaining oregano, season to taste wi salt and pepper and pour over the remaining cream. Scatter over the remaining cheese.

4 Cover with foil and bake in the preheated oven for 40 minutes, or until the parsnips are tender. Remove the foil and return to the oven for a further 5–10 minutes until the top is golden and bubbling. Serve.

★ Variation

This delicious casserole can be made with the same quantity of sliced celeriac instead of the parsnips and Gruyère cheese instead of Chedda

SIDES & SAUCES

PERFECT ROAST POTATOES

Serves: 8 **Prep: 25 mins** **Cook: 1 hour 25 mins**

Ingredients

- 70 g/2½ oz goose fat
- 1 tsp coarse sea salt
- 1 kg/2 lb 4 oz even-sized floury potatoes
- fresh rosemary sprigs, to garnish

Method

1. Preheat the oven to 230°C/450°F/Gas Mark 8. Put the fat in a large roasting tin, sprinkle generously with the salt and place in the preheated oven.
2. Meanwhile, bring a large saucepan of water t the boil, add the potatoes, bring back to the boil and cook for 8–10 minutes until parboiled Drain well and, if the potatoes are large, cut them in half. Return the potatoes to the empty pan and shake vigorously to roughen them on the outside.
3. Arrange the potatoes in a single layer in the hot fat and roast in the preheated oven for 45 minutes. If they look as if they are beginning to char around the edges, reduce the oven temperature to 200°C/400°F/Gas Mark 6. Turn the potatoes over and roast for a further 30 minutes until crisp. Garnish with rosemary sprig and serve immediately.

★ Variation

Toss the parboiled potatoes in a little English mustard powder to give an extra golden crust If you can't get goose fat, use the same quan of duck fat or 5 tablespoons of olive oil instea

LEMON & PAPRIKA HASSELBACK POTATOES

Makes: 12 **Prep: 15–20 mins** **Cook: 55 mins–1 hour**

Ingredients

12 waxy new potatoes, scrubbed and patted dry

30 g/1 oz butter, diced

3 tbsp lemon-flavoured olive oil

1 tsp coarse sea salt

½ tsp hot paprika

Yogurt-dill sauce

85 g/3 oz Greek-style yogurt

finely grated zest of 1 lemon

1 tbsp chopped fresh dill

salt and white pepper (optional)

Method

1 Preheat the oven to 220°C/425°F/Gas Mark 7. Cut 3-mm/⅛-inch slices all along the width of the potatoes, taking care not to cut right through (the potatoes should be in one piece).

2 On the hob over a high heat, melt the butter with the oil in a baking tray until sizzling. Stir in ½ teaspoon of the sea salt until it dissolves.

3 Turn off the heat and roll the potatoes in the buttery mixture. Use your fingers to crumble ove the remaining sea salt.

4 Roast the potatoes in the preheated oven for 3 minutes. Remove the tray from the oven and st the paprika into the oil, then baste the potatoe Use a spoon to get the oil between the slices.

5 Return the baking tray to the oven and contin roasting for a further 25–30 minutes, or until the potatoes are tender and browned.

6 Meanwhile, make the yogurt-dill sauce. In a bowl, mix the yogurt, lemon zest and 2 teaspoons of the dill together. Add salt and pepper to taste, if using. Cover and chill.

7 When the potatoes are tender, add a dollop o sauce on top of each one and sprinkle over th remaining dill.

MASHED SWEET POTATOES

Serves: 4 **Prep: 10 mins** **Cook: 25 mins, plus standing**

Ingredients

70 g/2½ oz butter, softened

2 tbsp chopped fresh parsley

900 g/2 lb sweet potatoes, scrubbed

Method

1. Reserving 30 g/1 oz, put the butter into a bowl with the parsley and beat together. Turn out the mixture onto a square of foil or clingfilm, shape into a block and transfer to the refrigerator to chill until required.
2. Cut the sweet potatoes into even-sized chunks. Bring a large saucepan of water to the boil, ad the sweet potatoes, bring back to the boil and cook, covered, for 15–20 minutes until tender.
3. Drain the potatoes well, then cover the pan with a clean tea towel and leave to stand for 2 minutes. Remove the skins and mash with a potato masher until fluffy.
4. Add the reserved butter to the potatoes and st in evenly. Spoon the mash into a serving dish and serve, topped with chunks of parsley butte

SPICED CARROT MASH

Serves: 4

Prep: 20 mins, plus cooling

Cook: 30–35 mins

Ingredients

1.25 kg/2 lb 12 oz carrots, cut in half lengthways

1 small bulb of garlic, cloves peeled

1 tsp ground turmeric

1 tsp ground coriander

1 tsp ground cumin

2 tbsp olive oil

salt and pepper (optional)

2 tsp black onion seeds and 1 tbsp roughly chopped fresh flat-leaf parsley, to garnish (optional)

Method

1. Preheat the oven to 200°C/400°F/Gas Mark 6.
2. Place the carrots, garlic cloves, turmeric, coriander and cumin in a large roasting tin. Drizzle over the oil and stir well until the carrots are coated thoroughly. Season with salt and pepper, if using.
3. Roast in the preheated oven for 30–35 minutes or until soft. Turn once, about halfway through, ensure even cooking.
4. Remove from the oven and leave to cool sligh Firmly mash the carrot mixture until you have c soft consistency, adding a touch of hot water i needed. Season again with salt and pepper tc taste, if using.
5. Serve immediately in a warmed serving dish, garnished with black onion seeds and parsley if using.

TWO POTATO PURÉE

Serves: 6 **Prep: 25 mins** **Cook: 20–25 mins**

Ingredients

2 large orange sweet potatoes, unpeeled

½ tsp vegetable oil

1–2 tsp salt

4 white potatoes, cut into large chunks

30 g/1 oz butter

125 ml/4 fl oz double cream

pinch of freshly grated nutmeg

salt and pepper (optional)

Method

1 Preheat the oven to 190°C/375°F/Gas Mark 5. Rub the sweet potatoes with the oil, then bake in the preheated oven for 20–25 minutes until tender.

2 Meanwhile, add 1–2 teaspoons of salt to a larg saucepan of water and bring to the boil, then add the white potatoes, bring back to the boil and cook until tender. Drain well and put in a colander. Cover with a clean tea towel to absc the steam. Mash the potatoes or pass through potato ricer into a warmed bowl.

3 Scoop out the flesh from the sweet potatoes a mix well with the white potato mash. Discard the sweet potato skins. Melt the butter with the cream in a small saucepan, then pour half ov the potato mixture and beat well with a wood spoon. Add the remaining cream mixture a little at a time until you achieve the consistenc you like. Season to taste with salt and pepper, using, and add a pinch of nutmeg. Beat agair then serve.

2
3

POTATO SALAD

Serves: 4–6

Prep: 20 mins, plus standing

Cook: 12 mins

Ingredients

1–2 tsp salt

900 g/2 lb small red-skinned salad potatoes, unpeeled

16–18 cornichons, halved diagonally

2 tbsp finely chopped red onion

3 tbsp snipped fresh chives

¼ tsp pepper

Mustard vinaigrette

2 tsp Dijon mustard

1 tbsp red wine vinegar

¼ tsp pepper

4 tbsp extra virgin olive oil

pinch of sea salt flakes

Method

1. Add 1–2 teaspoons of salt to a saucepan of water and bring to the boil. Add the potatoes, bring back to the boil and cook for 10–12 minutes until tender. Drain, then return to the po and leave for a few minutes.
2. To make the mustard vinaigrette, combine the mustard, vinegar, pepper and sea salt flakes in a bowl, mixing well. Add the oil and whisk until smooth and thickened.
3. Put the potatoes into a serving bowl and pour over the dressing. Add the remaining ingredier and toss gently to mix, then leave the salad to stand at room temperature for at least 30 minutes before serving.

PECAN-GLAZED BRUSSELS SPROUTS

Serves: 6 **Prep: 15 mins** **Cook: 25 mins**

Ingredients

- 650 g/1 lb 7 oz Brussels sprouts
- 125 ml/4 fl oz water
- 5 g/2 oz unsalted butter
- 70 g/2½ oz soft light brown sugar
- 3 tbsp soy sauce
- ¼ tsp salt
- g/2¼ oz finely chopped pecan nuts, toasted

Method

1. Cut off the stem ends of the sprouts and slash the base of each sprout with a shallow 'X'. Bring the water to the boil in a large saucepan, add the sprouts, cover, then reduce the heat and simmer for 8–10 minutes, or until the sprouts are slightly soft, then drain and set aside.
2. Melt the butter in a frying pan and stir in the sugar, soy sauce and salt. Bring to the boil, stirring constantly. Add the nuts, reduce the heat and simmer, uncovered, for 5 minutes, stirring occasionally. Add the sprouts and cook over a medium heat for 5 minutes. Stir well, transfer to a warmed serving dish and serve immediately.

STICKY CARROTS WITH WHISKY & GINGER GLAZE

Serves: 2–3 **Prep: 15 mins** **Cook: 20 mins**

Ingredients

1 tsp sugar

½ tsp pepper

good pinch of sea salt flakes

4 tbsp groundnut oil

40 g/1½ oz lightly salted butter

4 large carrots, sliced diagonally into 1-cm/½-inch rounds

2-cm/¾-inch piece fresh ginger, cut into batons

2 tbsp whisky

125 ml/4 fl oz chicken stock

Method

1 Mix the sugar, pepper and salt together in a bowl and set aside until needed.

2 Heat the oil with half the butter in a large frying pan. Add the carrots in a single layer and sprinkle with the sugar mixture. Cook over a medium–high heat for 3 minutes, then start turning the slices with tongs and reduce the heat if necessary. When brown on both sides and starting to blacken at the edges, transfer to a plate.

3 Wipe out the pan with kitchen paper. Add the ginger and cook over a medium–high heat for 1–2 minutes, until golden. Add to the carrots.

4 Add the remaining butter, the whisky and stock to the pan. Bring to the boil, then reduce the heat and simmer for 3 minutes or until syrupy. Return the carrots and ginger to the pan and swirl with the syrup for 1 minute. Serve immediately.

SPICED VEGETABLES

Serves: 4

Prep: 15–20 mins, plus resting & chilling

Cook: 1 hour 15 mins

Ingredients

4 parsnips, scrubbed and trimmed but left unpeeled

4 carrots, scrubbed and trimmed but left unpeeled

2 onions, quartered

1 red onion, quartered

3 leeks, trimmed and cut into 6-cm/2½-inch slices

6 garlic cloves, left unpeeled and whole

6 tbsp extra virgin olive oil

½ tsp mild chilli powder

pinch of paprika

salt and pepper (optional)

Method

1. Preheat the oven to 220°C/425°F/Gas Mark 7. Bring a large saucepan of water to the boil.
2. Cut the parsnips and carrots into wedges of similar size. Add them to the pan and cook for 5 minutes. Drain thoroughly and place in an ovenproof dish with the onions, leeks and garlic Pour over the oil, sprinkle in the spices and salt and pepper, if using, then mix until all the vegetables are well coated.
3. Roast in the preheated oven for at least 1 hour. Turn the vegetables from time to time until they are tender and starting to colour. Remove from the oven, transfer to a warmed serving dish and serve immediately.

SPROUTING BROCCOLI WITH PINE NUTS

Serves: 4 **Prep: 25 mins** **Cook: 20–25 mins**

Ingredients

700 g/1 lb 9 oz purple sprouting broccoli

3 tbsp extra virgin olive oil

3 shallots, thinly sliced

2 large garlic cloves, thinly sliced

pinch of red chilli flakes

3 tbsp pine nuts, toasted

55 g/2 oz butter

2 tbsp capers, drained

4 tbsp snipped fresh chives

30 g/1 oz Parmesan cheese, shaved into wafers

salt and pepper (optional)

Method

1 Cut off the broccoli florets and slice lengthways thick. Slice the leaves and stems into 2-cm/ ¾-inch pieces. Steam for 2 minutes over a saucepan of boiling water, until barely soft. Remove from the pan with a slotted spoon, reserving the cooking water.

2 Heat the oil in a large frying pan over a medium low heat. Add the shallots and fry for 5 minutes. Add the garlic and fry for 2–3 minutes, or until ju starting to colour.

3 Increase the heat to medium and add the broccoli to the pan. Add the chilli flakes and season with salt and pepper, if using. Add 3–4 tablespoons of the broccoli cooking water. Coo and keep stirring for 4–6 minutes, or until the broccoli is just tender and is still bright green.

4 Stir in the pine nuts and check the seasoning. Ti into a serving dish and keep warm.

5 Heat a heavy-based frying pan. When it is very hot, add the butter and sizzle until golden.

6 Remove from the heat and stir in the capers an half of the chives.

7 Pour the sauce over the broccoli. Sprinkle with the cheese shavings and the remaining chives.

BRAISED RED CABBAGE

Serves: 4 **Prep: 15 mins** **Cook: 50–55 mins**

Ingredients

- 30 g/1 oz butter
- 1 large red onion, thinly sliced
- 450 g/1 lb red cabbage, outer leaves removed
- 5 tbsp vegetable stock
- ¼ tsp ground cinnamon
- 5 juniper berries, lightly crushed
- finely grated rind and juice of ½ orange
- 2 tsp soft brown sugar
- 300 g/10½ oz firm ripe plums, stoned and halved or quartered if large
- salt and pepper (optional)

Method

1. Melt the butter in a saucepan. Add the onion, cover and cook gently for 5 minutes until soft. Meanwhile, quarter and core the cabbage and shred finely.
2. Add the cabbage to the pan with the stock, cinnamon, juniper berries, orange rind and juice and sugar. Mix well. Cover and cook over a low heat for 35 minutes.
3. Stir in the plums and season with salt and pepper, if using. Cover and cook for a further 10–12 minutes until tender. Serve immediately.

BUTTERED BRUSSELS SPROUTS WITH CHESTNUTS

Serves: 4 **Prep: 10 mins** **Cook: 15 mins**

Ingredients

1–2 tsp salt
350 g/12 oz Brussels sprouts
40 g/1½ oz butter
100 g/3½ oz canned whole chestnuts, drained
pinch of grated nutmeg
salt and pepper (optional)
50 g/1¾ oz flaked almonds, to garnish

Method

1 Add 1–2 teaspoons of salt to a large saucepan of water and bring to the boil. Add the Brussels sprouts and cook for 5 minutes. Drain thorough

2 Melt the butter in a large saucepan over a medium heat. Add the Brussels sprouts and cook, stirring, for 3 minutes, then add the chestnuts and nutmeg. Season to taste with sa and pepper, if using, and stir well. Cook for a further 2 minutes, stirring, then remove from the heat. Transfer to a warmed serving dish, scatter over the almonds and serve.

ROASTED ONIONS

'erves: 4 | Prep: 15 mins | Cook: 1 hour–1 hour 5 mins

Ingredients

8 large onions
3 tbsp olive oil
55 g/2 oz butter
o chopped fresh thyme
200 g/7 oz Cheddar cheese or Lancashire cheese, grated
and pepper (optional)

Method

1. Preheat the oven to 180°C/350°F/Gas Mark 4. Cut a cross down through the tops of the onions towards the root, without cutting all the way through. Place the onions in a roasting tin and drizzle over the oil.
2. Press a little of the butter into the open crosses, sprinkle with the thyme and season with salt and pepper, if using. Cover with foil and roast in the preheated oven for 40–45 minutes.
3. Remove from the oven, take off the foil and baste the onions with the pan juices. Return to the oven and cook for a further 15 minutes, uncovered, to allow the onions to brown.
4. Take the onions out of the oven and scatter the grated cheese over them. Return to the oven for a few minutes so that the cheese starts to melt. Serve immediately.

CAULIFLOWER CHEESE

Serves: 4 **Prep: 35 mins** **Cook: 50 mins**

Ingredients

1 tsp salt

1 head of cauliflower, cut into florets, 675 g/ 1 lb 8 oz prepared weight

40 g/1½ oz butter

40 g/1½ oz plain flour

475 ml/16 fl oz milk

115 g/4 oz Cheddar cheese, finely grated

pinch of freshly grated nutmeg

1 tbsp freshly grated Parmesan cheese

salt and pepper (optional)

Method

1 Add 1 teaspoon of salt to a large saucepan of water and bring to the boil. Add the cauliflowe bring back to the boil and cook for 4–5 minute It should still be firm. Drain, place in a warmed 1.5-litre/2½-pint gratin dish, set aside and keep warm.

2 Melt the butter in the rinsed-out pan over a medium heat and stir in the flour. Cook for 1 minute, stirring constantly. Remove from the he and gradually stir in the milk until smooth.

3 Return to a medium heat and continue to stir until the sauce comes to the boil and thickens Reduce the heat and gently simmer, stirring constantly, for about 3 minutes, until the sauce creamy and smooth.

4 Remove from the heat and stir in the Cheddar cheese and a good pinch of the grated nutmeg. Season to taste with salt and pepper, using.

5 Preheat the grill to high. Pour the sauce over th cauliflower, scatter over the Parmesan cheese and place under the preheated grill to brown. Serve immediately.

GARLIC MUSHROOMS WITH CHESTNUTS

Serves: 4 **Prep: 15 mins** **Cook: 15 mins**

Ingredients

- 55 g/2 oz butter
- 4 garlic cloves, chopped
- 200 g/7 oz button mushrooms, sliced
- 200 g/7 oz chestnut mushrooms, sliced
- 4 tbsp dry white wine
- 100 ml/3½ fl oz double cream
- 300 g/10½ oz canned whole chestnuts, drained
- 100 g/3½ oz chanterelle mushrooms, sliced
- salt and pepper (optional)
- chopped fresh parsley, to garnish

Method

1. Melt the butter in a large saucepan over a medium heat. Add the garlic and cook, stirring, for 3 minutes, until soft. Add the button mushrooms and chestnut mushrooms and cook for 3 minutes.
2. Stir in the wine and cream and season with salt and pepper, if using. Cook for 2 minutes, stirring, then add the chestnuts and the chanterelle mushrooms. Cook for a further 2 minutes, stirring, then remove from the heat and transfer to a warmed serving dish. Garnish with chopped fresh parsley and serve.

FRENCH BEAN CASSEROLE

Serves: 4–6 **Prep: 10 mins** **Cook: 40–45 mins**

Ingredients

500 g/1 lb 2 oz French beans, cut into 4-cm/1½-inch lengths

300 ml/10 fl oz canned condensed mushroom soup

225 ml/8 fl oz milk

1 tsp soy sauce

1 tbsp corn oil

15 g/½ oz butter

1 onion, sliced into rings

Method

1. Preheat the oven to 180°C/350°F/Gas Mark 4. Bring a saucepan of water to the boil and add the beans. Bring back to the boil and cook for 5 minutes. Drain well.
2. Put the soup, milk and soy sauce into a bowl and mix together, then stir in the beans. Tip into a 1.5-litre/2½-pint casserole and distribute evenly. Bake in the preheated oven for 25–30 minutes, until bubbling and golden.
3. Meanwhile, heat the oil and butter in a frying pan, add the onion rings and fry over a fairly high heat, stirring frequently, until golden brown and crisp. Remove and drain on absorbent kitchen paper.
4. Arrange the onion rings on top of the casserole and bake for a further 5 minutes. Serve hot.

SUGAR-GLAZED PARSNIPS

Serves: 8 **Prep: 5 mins** **Cook: 50 mins**

Ingredients

24 small parsnips, halved
1 tsp salt
115 g/4 oz butter
115 g/4 oz soft light brown sugar

Method

1. Place the parsnips in a saucepan, add just enough water to cover, then add the salt. Bring to the boil, reduce the heat, cover and simmer for 20–25 minutes, until tender. Drain well.
2. Melt the butter in a heavy frying pan or wok. Add the parsnips and toss well. Sprinkle with the sugar, then cook, stirring frequently to prevent the sugar sticking to the pan or burning for 10–15 minutes until golden and glazed. Transfer the parsnips to a warmed serving dish and serve immediately.

BACON-WRAPPED SAUSAGES

Makes: 8 **Prep: 15 mins** **Cook: 15–20 mins**

Ingredients

8 pork sausages
2 tbsp mild mustard
24 ready-to-eat prunes
8 smoked bacon rashers

Method

1 Preheat the grill. Using a sharp knife, cut a slit along the length of each sausage about three quarters of the way through. Spread the musta inside the slits and press 3 prunes into each sausage.

2 Stretch the bacon with the back of a knife unti each rasher is quite thin. Wrap a rasher of bac around each sausage.

3 Place the sausages on a grill rack and cook under the grill, turning occasionally, for 15–20 minutes until cooked through and brown all ov

FESTIVE JEWELLED RICE

Serves: 6 **Prep: 30 mins** **Cook: 15–20 mins**

Ingredients

- 250 g/9 oz basmati rice
- 70 g/2½ oz red or wild rice
- 70 g /2½ oz ready-to-eat dried apricots
- 30 g/1 oz blanched almonds
- 30 g/1 oz hazelnuts, toasted
- 1 fresh red chilli, deseeded and finely chopped
- seeds of 1 pomegranate
- 1 tbsp finely chopped fresh parsley
- 1 tbsp finely chopped fresh mint
- 1 tbsp finely snipped fresh chives
- 2 tbsp white wine vinegar
- 6 tbsp extra virgin olive oil
- 1 shallot, finely chopped
- salt and pepper (optional)

Method

1. Cook the basmati rice and red rice separately according to the packet instructions. Drain and leave to cool, then tip into a large bowl.
2. Chop the apricots, almonds and hazelnuts and add to the rice with the chilli, pomegranate seeds, parsley, mint and chives. Mix well togethe
3. Just before you are ready to serve, whisk together the vinegar, oil and shallot in a jug anc season with salt and pepper, if using. Pour the dressing over the rice and mix well. Pile into a large bowl and serve.

MAKE-AHEAD GRAVY FOR ROAST TURKEY

Serves: 4 **Prep: 10–15 mins** **Cook: 40–50 mins**

Ingredients

- 2 tbsp sunflower oil
- 2 carrots, peeled and diced
- 2 celery sticks, diced
- 2 shallots, finely chopped
- pinch of salt
- 4 tbsp plain flour
- 1 litre/1¾ pints turkey stock or chicken stock, simmering
- 4 fresh parsley sprigs, chopped
- 2 fresh thyme sprigs
- pan juices from roasting the turkey
- salt and pepper (optional)

Method

1. Heat the sunflower oil in a heavy-based saucepan over a medium heat. Stir in the carrots, celery, shallots and salt, then reduce the heat to low. Cover the surface of the vegetables with a piece of wet greaseproof paper cut to fit, cover the pan and leave the vegetables to sweat for 10 minutes, or until very tender.
2. Stir the flour into the pan, increase the heat slightly and stir for 3 minutes to cook out the flour's raw flavour. The mixture will be very thick and glue-like.
3. Slowly pour the stock into the pan, stirring to avoid any lumps. Add the parsley and thyme and bring to the boil. Reduce the heat to very low, skim the surface and leave to simmer for 20–30 minutes to concentrate the flavours, or until reduced to 500 ml/17 fl oz.
4. Strain the stock into a bowl, pressing down on the vegetables to extract as much flavour as possible. Discard the vegetables. Leave the gravy to cool completely, then cover and chill for up to 2 days, or freeze for up to 1 month. Thaw thoroughly before reheating.

When ready to serve with the roast turkey, transfer the gravy to a saucepan and bring to the boil. Reduce the heat to low and leave to simmer as the turkey finishes roasting.

While the turkey is resting, very carefully pour the pan juices into a jug. Stir the juices into the stock, then continue simmering until it is time to serve. Add salt and pepper, if using, but bear in mind that the juices might be very salty.

Pour the gravy into a warmed gravy boat and serve immediately.

RICH ONION GRAVY

Serves: 8 **Prep: 15 mins** **Cook: 1 hour 25 mins**

Ingredients

- 2 tbsp sunflower oil
- 450 g/1 lb onions, thinly sliced
- 2 garlic cloves, crushed
- 1 tbsp sugar
- 30 g/1 oz plain flour
- 150 ml/5 fl oz red wine
- 600 ml/1 pint boiling beef stock
- 2 tsp Dijon mustard
- pinch of gravy browning (optional)
- salt and pepper (optional)

Method

1. Heat the oil in a large, heavy-based saucepan. Add the onions, garlic and sugar and fry over a low heat for 30 minutes, stirring occasionally, until very soft and light golden in colour.
2. Stir in the flour and cook for 1 minute. Add the wine and bring to the boil, then simmer and beat until the mixture is smooth. Add 150 ml/ 5 fl oz of the stock and bring back to the boil. Simmer and beat again to mix thoroughly.
3. Stir in the remaining stock, mustard and gravy browning, if using. Bring back to the boil and season with salt and pepper, if using.
4. Simmer for 20 minutes, then pour into a warmed gravy boat and serve immediately.

CRANBERRY SAUCE

Serves: 8 **Prep: 20 mins** **Cook: 5 mins**

Ingredients

- thinly pared rind and juice of 1 lemon
- thinly pared rind and juice of 1 orange
- 350 g/12 oz cranberries, thawed if frozen
- 140 g/5 oz caster sugar
- 2 tbsp arrowroot, mixed with 3 tbsp cold water

Method

1. Put the lemon rind and orange rind into a heavy-based saucepan. If using fresh cranberries, rinse well and remove any stalks. Add the berries, lemon juice, orange juice and sugar to the pan and cook over a medium he stirring occasionally, for 5 minutes, or until the berries begin to burst.
2. Strain the juice into a clean saucepan and reserve the cranberries. Stir the arrowroot mixture into the juice, then bring to the boil, stirring constantly, until the sauce is smooth an thickened. Remove from the heat and stir in the reserved cranberries. Discard the pieces of lemon and orange rind.
3. Transfer the cranberry sauce to a bowl and leave to cool, then cover with clingfilm and ch in the refrigerator until ready to use.

RICH BREAD SAUCE

erves: 12

Prep: 15 mins, plus infusing

Cook: 20–25 mins

Ingredients

- 1 onion, peeled but left whole
- 12 cloves
- 1 bay leaf
- 6 peppercorns
- 600 ml/1 pint milk
- 115 g/4 oz fresh white breadcrumbs
- 30 g/1 oz butter
- ½ tsp grated nutmeg
- 2 tbsp double cream (optional)
- and pepper (optional)
- freshly grated nutmeg d 1 bay leaf, to garnish

Method

1. Make 12 small holes in the onion using a skewer or sharp knife and stick a clove in each hole.
2. Place the onion, bay leaf and peppercorns in a small saucepan and pour in the milk. Bring to the boil over a medium heat, then remove from the heat, cover and leave to infuse for 1 hour.
3. Strain the milk and discard the onion, bay leaf and peppercorns.
4. Return the milk to the rinsed-out pan and add the breadcrumbs. Cook the sauce over a very gentle heat until the breadcrumbs have swollen and the sauce is thick. Stir in the butter and season with salt and pepper, if using.
5. When ready to serve, reheat the sauce briefly, if necessary. Add the nutmeg and stir in the cream, if using. Pour into a warmed serving bowl and serve immediately, garnished with a bay leaf and grated nutmeg.

CORN RELISH

Makes: 600 g/ 1 lb 5 oz **Prep: 20 mins** **Cook: 20 mins**

Ingredients

1-2 tsp salt
5 corn cobs, husks and silks removed
1 red pepper, deseeded and finely diced
2 celery sticks, very finely chopped
1 red onion, finely chopped
125 g/4½ oz sugar
1 tbsp salt
2 tbsp mustard powder
½ tsp celery seeds
¼ tsp turmeric (optional)
225 ml/8 fl oz cider vinegar
125 ml/4 fl oz water

Method

1. Add 1–2 teaspoons of salt to a large saucepan of water and bring to the boil. Fill a bowl with iced water. Add the corn to the boiling water, bring back to the boil and boil for 2 minutes, or until the kernels are tender-crisp. Using tongs, immediately plunge the cobs into the cold water to halt cooking. Remove from the water, cut the kernels from the cobs, then set aside.
2. Add the red pepper, celery and onion to the corn cooking water, bring back to the boil and boil for 2 minutes, or until tender-crisp. Drain well and return to the pan with the corn kernels.
3. Put the sugar, salt, mustard, celery seeds and turmeric, if using, into a bowl and mix together, then stir in the vinegar and water. Add to the pan, bring the liquid to the boil, then reduce the heat and simmer for 15 minutes, stirring occasionally.
4. Ladle the relish into hot, sterilized preserving jars, filling them to within 1 cm/½ inch of the top of each jar. Wipe the rims and secure the lids. Leave the relish to cool completely, then refrigerate for up to 2 months.

SAGE, ONION & APPLE STUFFING

Serves: 10 **Prep: 20 mins** **Cook: 20–25 mins**

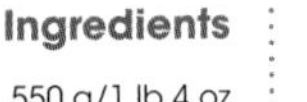

Ingredients

550 g/1 lb 4 oz pork sausage meat
1 onion, grated
350 g/12 oz cooking apple, peeled, cored and finely chopped
30 g/1 oz fresh white breadcrumbs
2 tbsp chopped fresh sage or marjoram
grated rind of 1 lemon
1 egg, beaten
vegetable oil, for oiling
salt and pepper (optional)
sage sprig, to garnish

Method

1 Preheat the oven to 190°C/375°F/Gas Mark 5. Place the sausage meat, onion, apple, breadcrumbs, sage, lemon rind and egg in a large bowl. Season to taste with salt and peppe if using, and mix until thoroughly combined.

2 Shape the stuffing into balls, place on an oiled baking sheet and bake in the preheated oven for 25 minutes. Garnish with a sprig of sage anc serve immediately.

3 Alternatively, place the stuffing mixture in a 900-g/2-lb loaf tin, level the surface and bake ir the preheated oven for 50 minutes.

4 It is safer and more reliable to cook the stuffing separately, but if you prefer to stuff a turkey or goose, fill the neck cavity only to ensure the bird cooks all the way through. To calculate th cooking time correctly, weigh the bird after it h been stuffed.

MIXED MUSHROOM & CHESTNUT STUFFING

Serves: 6

Prep: 20 mins, plus soaking & cooling

Cook: 40–45 mins

Ingredients

175 ml/6 fl oz boiling water
85 g/3 oz dried porcini mushrooms
250 g/9 oz day-old light rye bread
2 tsp olive oil, for oiling
2 tbsp olive oil
4 celery stalks, chopped
1 large leek, trimmed, quartered and sliced
2 garlic cloves, chopped
500 g/1 lb 2 oz chestnut mushrooms, quartered and thinly sliced
½ tsp salt
1 tsp dried sage
4 fresh thyme sprigs, leaves separated
1 egg, beaten
125 g/4½ oz peeled, cooked chestnuts, chopped
5 tbsp dried cranberries
4 tbsp chopped fresh parsley
1 tbsp chopped fresh parsley, to garnish
pepper (optional)

Method

1 Pour the boiling water over the dried mushroom and leave them to soak for at least 20 minutes, or until tender. Strain the mushrooms through a sieve lined with muslin or a coffee filter, then reserve the mushrooms and soaking liquid in separate bowls.

2 Preheat the oven to 200°C/400°F/Gas Mark 6. Cut or tear the bread into 5-mm/¼-inch pieces and put them into a large mixing bowl. Oil a 28 x 18-cm/11 x 7-inch ovenproof serving bowl. Set the mixing bowl and ovenproof bowl aside.

3 Heat the oil in a large frying pan over a mediun heat. Add the celery and leek, and fry, stirring occasionally, for 3–5 minutes until soft. Add the garlic and stir for a further 2 minutes.

4 Add the soaked mushrooms, chestnut mushrooms, salt, sage, thyme and pepper to taste, if using. Stir for 10 minutes, or until the mushrooms are tender and have re-absorbed their liquid. Leave to cool slightly, then stir in the egg, followed by the chestnuts, cranberries anc chopped parsley.

5 Gently stir this mixture into the bowl with the bread. Very gradually add just enough of the mushroom soaking liquid to moisten the bread It should not be soggy.

Spoon the stuffing into the ovenproof bowl. Place in the oven and roast for 20–25 minutes until the stuffing is piping hot. Garnish with chopped parsley and serve immediately.

CHESTNUT & SAUSAGE STUFFING

Serves: 6–8 **Prep: 10 mins** **Cook: 30–40 mins**

Ingredients

- 225 g/8 oz pork sausage meat
- 225 g/8 oz unsweetened chestnut purée
- 85 g/3 oz walnuts, chopped
- 115 g/4 oz ready-to-eat dried apricots, chopped
- 2 tbsp chopped fresh parsley
- 2 tbsp snipped fresh chives
- 2 tsp chopped fresh sage
- 4–5 tbsp double cream
- salt and pepper (optional)

Method

1 Preheat the oven to 190°C/375°F/Gas Mark 5. Combine the sausage meat and chestnut purée in a bowl, then stir in the walnuts, apricot parsley, chives and sage. Stir in enough cream to make a firm, but not dry, mixture. Season to taste with salt and pepper, if using.

2 If you are planning to stuff a turkey or goose, fill the neck cavity only to ensure the bird cooks all the way through. It is safer and more reliable to cook the stuffing separately, either rolled into small balls and placed on a baking sheet or spooned into an ovenproof dish.

3 Cook the separate stuffing in a preheated oven for 30–40 minutes at 190°C/375°F/Gas Mark 5. I should be allowed a longer time to cook if you are roasting a bird at a lower temperature in th same oven.

MANGO & MACADAMIA STUFFING

Serves: 4–6 **Prep: 10 mins** **Cook: 30 mins**

Ingredients

- 10 g/¼ oz butter, for greasing
- 30 g/1 oz butter
- 1 small onion, finely chopped
- 1 celery stick, diced
- 175 g/6 oz fresh white breadcrumbs
- 1 egg, beaten
- 1 tbsp Dijon mustard
- 1 small mango, peeled, stoned and diced
- 85 g/3 oz macadamia nuts, chopped
- salt and pepper (optional)

Method

1. Preheat the oven to 200°C/400°F/Gas Mark 6. Grease a 750-ml/1¼-pint ovenproof dish.
2. Melt the butter in a saucepan, add the onion and fry, stirring, for 3–4 minutes, until soft. Add the celery and cook for a further 2 minutes.
3. Remove from the heat and stir in the breadcrumbs, egg and mustard. Add the mango and nuts, then season with salt and pepper, if using.
4. Spread the mixture in the prepared dish and bake in the preheated oven for 20–25 minutes, until golden and bubbling.

★ Variation

Apricots are a good substitute for mango in this recipe. Soak 100 g/3½ oz ready-to-eat-dried apricots in warm water for 30 minutes, then drain, chop and add in step 3.

DESSERTS AND DRINKS

CHRISTMAS PAVLOVA WREATH

Serves: 14

Prep: 30 mins, plus cooling

Cook: 50 mins–1 hour

Ingredients

- 15 g/½ oz butter, softened, for greasing
- 1 tbsp plain flour, for dusting
- 6 large egg whites, at room temperature
- ½ tsp cream of tartar
- 350 g/12 oz caster sugar
- ½ tsp vanilla extract
- 1½ tsp cornflour
- 1½ tsp white wine vinegar

To decorate

- 450 ml/15 fl oz double cream
- 2 tbsp orange-flavoured liqueur
- 2 tbsp icing sugar
- 85 g/3 oz raspberries
- 85 g/3 oz blueberries
- 85 g/3 oz strawberries, halved
- 8 fresh mint sprigs

Method

1. Preheat the oven to 150°C/300°F/Gas Mark 2. Line a baking tray with baking paper and mark a 29-cm/11½-inch circle on the paper. Mark a 15-cm/6-inch circle in the centre. Turn the paper over so that the marked side is facing down. Very lightly grease the paper within the two lines then lightly dust with flour. Set aside.
2. Beat the egg whites in a large, clean, grease-free bowl until they hold soft peaks. Beat in the cream of tartar. Beat in the sugar, a few tablespoons at a time, until glossy and holding stiff peaks. Whisk in the vanilla extract with the final addition of sugar. Sift in the cornflour and fold in the vinegar.
3. Drop large spoonfuls of the meringue on the baking paper, filling in between the lines to form a wreath shape. Use the back of the spoon to create an indentation all around the circle.
4. Place in the preheated oven, immediately reduce the heat to 120°C/250°F/Gas ½, then bake for 50–60 minutes until the meringue is crisp when lightly tapped but still white. Turn off the oven and leave the meringue inside, with the door closed, for 2–3 minutes. Remove from the oven, lift off the baking paper and transfer the meringue to a serving platter.

Meanwhile, whisk the cream with the orange-flavoured liqueur until starting to thicken. Sift over the icing sugar and continue whisking until soft peaks form and the cream has a spreading consistency. Cover and chill until required. Spread the cream over the top of the wreath. Scatter with the fresh fruit. Add the sprigs of mint to decorate.

Variation

For a healthier version, replace half the double cream with Greek-style yogurt, and replace the orange-flavoured liqueur with vanilla bean paste.

CHEESECAKE WITH CARAMEL PECAN NUTS

Serves: 6–8

Prep: 25 mins

Cook: 1 hour 20 mins–1 hour 30 mins

Ingredients

Base

50 g/1¾ oz pecan nuts

150 g/5½ oz digestive biscuits, broken into pieces

50 g/1¾ oz butter, melted

Filling

400 g/14 oz cream cheese

200 g/7 oz curd cheese

125 g/4½ oz unrefined caster sugar

3 large eggs

3 large egg yolks

200 ml/7 fl oz double cream

Topping

10 g/¼ oz butter, for greasing

225 g/8 oz unrefined caster sugar

5 tbsp water

70 g/2½ oz pecan nuts

Method

1 Preheat the oven to 160°C/325°F/Gas Mark 3. T make the base, put the nuts in a food process and process briefly, then add the broken biscu and pulse again until crumbs form.

2 Tip into a bowl and stir in the melted butter until well combined. Press into the base of a 20-cm/8-inch round springform cake tin. Bake i the preheated oven for 10 minutes, then remov from the oven and leave to cool.

3 To make the filling, beat together the cream cheese, curd cheese and sugar in a large bow Beat in the eggs and egg yolks, one at a time, until smooth. Finally, stir in the cream. Spoon ov the prepared base.

4 Bake in the preheated oven for 1 hour, then tes – the cheesecake should be cooked but with slight 'wobble' in the centre. Return to the oven for a further 10 minutes if necessary. Remove from the oven and leave to cool in the tin.

5 To make the topping, grease a piece of foil wit butter and lay it flat. Put the sugar and water ir a saucepan and heat gently, stirring, until the sugar has dissolved.

Bring to a simmer, swirling the saucepan rather than stirring, and cook until the syrup begins to darken, then add the pecan nuts.

Transfer each nut to the greased foil and leave to harden. When you are ready to serve, unclip and remove the springform and turn out the cheesecake onto a serving plate. Arrange the caramel pecan nuts on top.

FESTIVE SHERRY TRIFLE

Serves: 4–6

Prep: 30 mins, plus standing & chilling

Cook: 20 mins

Ingredients

- 100 g/3½ oz trifle sponges, halved
- 2 tbsp raspberry jam, for spreading
- 150 ml/5 fl oz sherry
- 150 g/5½ oz frozen raspberries, thawed
- 350 g/12 oz fresh strawberries, sliced

Custard

- 6 egg yolks
- 50 g/1¾ oz caster sugar
- 500 ml/17 fl oz milk
- 1 tsp vanilla extract

Topping

- 300 ml/10 fl oz double cream
- 1–2 tbsp caster sugar
- 1 flaky chocolate bar, crumbled

Method

1. Spread the trifle sponges with jam, cut them in[to] bite-sized cubes and arrange in the base of a large glass serving bowl. Pour over the sherry and leave to stand for 30 minutes.
2. Combine the raspberries and strawberries and spoon them over the sponges in the bowl.
3. To make the custard, put the egg yolks and sugar into a bowl and whisk together. Pour the milk into a saucepan and heat over a low hea[t] until warm. Remove from the heat and gradua[lly] stir into the egg mixture, then return the mixture to the pan and stir constantly over a low heat until thickened. Do not boil. Remove from the heat, pour into a bowl and stir in the vanilla extract. Leave to cool for 1 hour. Spread the custard over the fruit, cover with clingfilm and chill in the refrigerator for 2 hours.
4. To make the topping, whip the cream in a bow[l] and stir in the sugar to taste. Spread the crea[m] over the trifle, then scatter over the chocolate pieces. Chill in the refrigerator for 30 minutes before serving.

APPLE PIE

Serves: 6

Prep: 40 mins, plus chilling

Cook: 50 mins

Ingredients

- 350 g/12 oz plain flour
- pinch of salt
- 85 g/3 oz butter or margarine, diced
- 85 g/3 oz lard or white vegetable fat, diced
- 6 tbsp cold water
- 10 g/¼ oz plain flour, for dusting
- 1 tbsp milk, for glazing

Filling

- 750 g–1 kg/1 lb 10 oz–2 lb 4oz cooking apples, peeled, cored and sliced
- 125 g/4½ oz caster sugar
- ½–1 tsp ground cinnamon, mixed spice, or ground ginger
- 1–2 tbsp water
- 10 g/¼ oz caster sugar, for sprinkling

Method

1. Sift the flour and salt into a mixing bowl. Add th butter and lard and rub in with your fingertips until the mixture resembles fine breadcrumbs.
2. Add the water and gather the mixture togethe into a dough. Wrap the dough in clingfilm and chill in the refrigerator for 30 minutes.
3. Preheat the oven to 220°C/425°F/Gas Mark 7. Thinly roll out almost two thirds of the pastry on a lightly floured surface and use to line a deep 23-cm/9-inch pie dish.
4. To make the filling, put the apple slices, sugar and spice into a bowl and mix well together. Pack the apple mixture into the pastry case; the filling can come up above the rim. Add the water, if needed, particularly if the apples are not very juicy.
5. Roll out the remaining pastry on a lightly floure surface to make a lid. Dampen the edges of th pie rim with water and position the lid, pressing the edges firmly together.
6. Trim and crimp the edges. Use the trimmings to cut out leaves or other shapes to decorate the top of the pie. Dampen and attach.

Glaze the top of the pie with milk, make two slits in the top and place the pie dish on a baking sheet.

Bake in the preheated oven for 20 minutes, then reduce the oven temperature to 180°C/350°F/Gas Mark 4 and bake for a further 30 minutes, or until the pastry is a light golden brown. Serve hot or cold, sprinkled with a little sugar.

PEPPERMINT CHEESECAKE

Serves: 12

Prep: 25 mins, plus cooling & chilling

Cook: 1 hour–1 hour 10 mins

Ingredients

900 g/2 lb full-fat cream cheese, at room temperature

200 g/7 oz caster sugar

4½ tsp peppermint extract

½ tsp pink food colouring paste

4 eggs, at room temperature

85 g/3 oz candy canes, finely crushed, to decorate

Chocolate crumb base

175 g/6 oz dark chocolate digestive biscuits

1 tbsp cocoa powder

85 g/3 oz butter, melted

⅛ tsp vanilla extract

Method

1. Preheat the oven to 150°C/300°F/Gas Mark 2.
2. To make the base, break the biscuits into a food processor and blitz until fine crumbs form. Add the cocoa powder and blitz until combined. Add the butter and vanilla extract and continu blitzing until blended.
3. Spread the crumb mixture over the base of a 23-cm/9-inch round non-stick springform cake tin. Set aside on a baking sheet.
4. Beat the cream cheese until softened, then add the sugar, peppermint extract and food colouring. Beat together until the sugar dissolv the cream cheese is smooth and fluffy and the colour is evenly distributed. Lightly beat in the eggs, one at a time.
5. Pour the cream cheese mixture on top of the base and smooth the surface. Bake in the preheated oven for 1 hour–1 hour 10 minutes until set around the edge but still slightly wobb in the centre. It will finish baking as it cools.
6. Turn off the oven and leave the cheesecake inside for 30 minutes with the door slightly ajar. Run a metal spatula around the inside of the t then transfer to a wire rack and leave to cool ir the tin.

When the cheesecake is completely cool, cover with clingfilm and chill for at least 8 hours.

When ready to serve, unclip and release the springform. Sprinkle the crushed candy canes around the rim of the cheesecake. Cover with a sheet of clingfilm and press the crumbs into the cheesecake. Remove the clingfilm and cut into 12 slices.

CRANBERRY & APPLE MERINGUES

Serves: 4 **Prep: 10 mins** **Cook: 20 mins**

Ingredients

500 g/1 lb cooking apples or firm eating apples

1 tbsp apple juice

175 g/6 oz caster sugar

100 g/3½ oz dried cranberries

2 egg whites

Method

1 Preheat the oven to 200°C/400°F/Gas Mark 6. Peel, core and chop the apples, place in a saucepan and sprinkle with the apple juice.

2 Add 70 g/2½ oz of the sugar and the cranberries, stir and heat gently until boiling. Cover the pan, reduce the heat and simmer gently, stirring occasionally, for 8–10 minutes, ur the fruit is just tender.

3 Divide the fruit between four 350-ml/12-fl oz ovenproof dishes and place on a baking shee

4 Put the egg whites into a clean, grease-free bo and whisk until they hold soft peaks. Gradually whisk in the remaining sugar until the mixture holds stiff peaks.

5 Spoon the meringue on top of the fruit, swirling with a knife. Bake in the preheated oven for 10-12 minutes, until the meringue is lightly browne Serve warm.

RICE PUDDING WITH CINNAMON-POACHED PLUMS

Serves: 4 **Prep: 15 mins** **Cook: 50–55 mins**

Ingredients

- 85 g/3 oz pudding rice
- 25 g/1 oz caster sugar
- g/½ oz unsalted butter
- 500 ml/17 fl oz milk
- zest of 1 orange

Compote

- 500 g/1 lb red plums, stoned and halved
- 1 cinnamon stick
- sp golden caster sugar
- juice of 1 orange

Method

1. Put the rice, sugar and butter into a saucepan and stir in the milk and half the orange zest. Heat gently, stirring occasionally, until almost boiling.
2. Reduce the heat to low, then cover and simmer gently for 40–45 minutes, stirring occasionally, until the rice is tender and most of the liquid has been absorbed.
3. Meanwhile, to make the compote, put the plums, cinnamon, sugar and orange juice into a large saucepan. Heat gently until just boiling, then reduce the heat, cover and simmer for about 10 minutes, or until the plums are tender.
4. Remove the plums with a slotted spoon and discard the cinnamon. Serve the rice pudding warm with the compote and sprinkle with the remaining orange zest.

TROPICAL FRUIT DESSERT

Serves: 6 **Prep: 20 mins** **Cook: No cooking**

Ingredients

14 amaretti biscuits

3 tbsp white rum

100 ml/3½ fl oz orange juice

1 papaya, halved, deseeded, peeled and chopped

½ small pineapple, peeled cored and chopped

2 kiwi fruit, peeled and chopped

300 ml/10 fl oz whipping cream

1 tsp vanilla extract

1 tbsp toasted flaked coconut, to decorate

Method

1. Roughly crumble the amaretti into a glass serving bowl and sprinkle with the rum and orange juice.
2. Mix together the papaya, pineapple and kiwi fruit and spread the mixture over the amaretti.
3. Whisk the cream with the vanilla extract until it just holds its shape, then spoon it over the fruit.
4. Scatter the toasted coconut over the cream. Serve chilled.

RICH CHOCOLATE PIES

Serves: 8

Prep: 20 mins, plus chilling

Cook: 35 mins

Ingredients

- 225 g/8 oz plain flour
- 115 g/4 oz butter, diced
- 2 tbsp icing sugar
- 1 egg yolk
- 2–3 tbsp cold water
- 10 g/¼ oz flour, for dusting

Filling

- 250 g/9 oz plain chocolate, broken into pieces
- 115 g/4 oz butter
- 50 g/1¾ oz icing sugar
- 300 ml/10 fl oz double cream
- grated chocolate, to decorate

Method

1. Sift the flour into a large bowl. Add the butter and rub it in with your fingertips until the mixture resembles breadcrumbs. Add the sugar, egg yolk and enough water to form a soft dough.
2. Wrap the dough in clingfilm and chill in the refrigerator for 15 minutes. Roll out the pastry on a lightly floured surface and use to line eight 10-cm/4-inch shallow tartlet tins. Chill in the refrigerator for 30 minutes.
3. Preheat the oven to 200°C/400°F/Gas Mark 6. Prick the cases with a fork and line with crumpled foil. Bake in the preheated oven for 10 minutes, then remove the foil and bake for a further 5–10 minutes.
4. Transfer to a wire rack to cool. Reduce the oven temperature to 160°C/325°F/Gas Mark 3.
5. To make the filling, place the chocolate, butter and sugar in a heatproof bowl set over a saucepan of gently simmering water and heat until melted. Remove from the heat and stir in 200 ml/7 fl oz of the cream.
6. Remove the pastry cases from the tins and place on a baking sheet. Fill each case with some of the chocolate mixture.

Return to the oven and bake for 5 minutes. Remove from the oven and leave to cool, then chill until required.

Whip the remaining cream and pipe into the centre of each tart. Decorate with grated chocolate and serve.

RICH CHRISTMAS PUDDING

Serves: 10

Prep: 30 mins,
plus soaking

Cook: 6 hours,
plus reheating

Ingredients

- 200 g/7 oz currants
- 200 g/7 oz raisins
- 200 g/7 oz sultanas
- 150 ml/5 fl oz sweet sherry
- 175 g/6 oz butter
- 175 g/6 oz brown sugar
- 4 eggs, beaten
- 150 g/5½ oz self-raising flour
- 100 g/3½ oz fresh breadcrumbs
- 50 g/1¾ oz blanched almonds, chopped
- juice of 1 orange
- grated rind of ½ orange
- grated rind of ½ lemon
- ½ tsp mixed spice
- 10 g/¼ oz butter, for greasing
- 10 g/¼ oz icing sugar, for dusting

Method

1 Put the currants, raisins and sultanas in a glass bowl and pour the sherry over. Cover and leave to soak for at least 2 hours.

2 Beat together the butter and brown sugar in a bowl. Beat in the eggs, then fold in the flour. Stir in the soaked fruit and the sherry with the breadcrumbs, almonds, orange juice, orange rind, lemon rind and mixed spice. Grease a 1.2-litre/2-pint pudding basin and spoon the mixture into it, packing it down well and leaving a gap of 2.5 cm/1 inch at the top. Cut a round of greaseproof paper 3 cm/1½ inches larger than the circumference of the top of the basin, grease with butter and place over the pudding. Secure with string, then top with two layers of foil.

3 Place the pudding in a saucepan two-thirds filled with boiling water. Reduce the heat and simmer for 6 hours, topping up the water in the saucepan when necessary.

4 Remove from the heat and leave to cool. Replace the greaseproof paper and foil and store the pudding in a cool place for 2–8 weeks. To reheat, steam as before for 2 hours. Decorate with a dusting of icing sugar and serve.

BOOZY CHOCOLATE CHEESECAKE

Serves: 8

Prep: 30 mins, plus chilling

Cook: 10 mins

Ingredients

1 tbsp vegetable oil, for oiling

175 g/6 oz chocolate chip cookies

55 g/2 oz unsalted butter

crème fraîche and fresh fruit, to serve (optional)

Filling

225 g/8 oz plain chocolate, broken into pieces

225 g/8 oz milk chocolate, broken into pieces

55 g/2 oz golden caster sugar

350 g/12 oz cream cheese

450 ml/15 fl oz double cream, lightly whipped

3 tbsp Irish cream liqueur

Method

1. Line the base of a 20-cm/8-inch round springform cake tin with baking paper and brush the sides with oil. Place the cookies in a polythene bag and crush with a rolling pin. Put the butter in a saucepan and gently heat until melted. Stir in the crushed cookies. Press into the base of the prepared tin and chill in the refrigerator for 1 hour.
2. Put the plain chocolate and milk chocolate into a heatproof bowl set over a saucepan of gently simmering water and heat until melted. Remove from the heat and leave to cool. Put the sugar and cream cheese into a bowl and beat together until smooth, then fold in the cream. Fold the melted chocolate into the cream cheese mixture, then stir in the liqueur.
3. Spoon the mixture into the tin and smooth the surface. Chill in the refrigerator for 2 hours, or until quite firm. Unclip and remove the springform, transfer the cheesecake to a serving plate and cut into slices. Serve with crème fraîche and fresh fruit, if using.

PROSECCO & LEMON SORBET

Serves: 4

Prep: 10 mins, plus freezing

Cook: 5 mins

Ingredients

- 140 g/5 oz caster sugar
- 100 ml/3½ fl oz water
- finely grated rind and juice of 1 lemon
- 350 ml/12 fl oz prosecco
- 4 fresh mint sprigs, to decorate

Method

1. Put the sugar and water into a saucepan with the grated lemon rind and stir over a low heat until the sugar dissolves.
2. Bring to the boil, then boil for 1 minute until slightly reduced. Leave to cool, then strain through a sieve.
3. Add the lemon juice and prosecco to the lemon syrup and stir to combine, then pour into an ice-cream maker and churn according to the manufacturer's instructions. Alternatively, pour into a freezer-proof container and place in the freezer. Remove from the freezer and whisk once an hour until completely frozen.
4. Remove the sorbet from the freezer about 15 minutes before serving, then scoop into serving dishes. Decorate with the mint sprigs and serve.

POACHED PEARS

Serves: 6

Prep: 20 mins, plus chilling & cooling

Cook: 50 mins– 1 hour 5 mins

Ingredients

6 dessert pears, peeled but left whole with stalks attached

500 ml/17 fl oz Marsala

125 ml/4 fl oz water

1 tbsp soft brown sugar

1 piece of lemon rind or mandarin rind

1 vanilla pod

350 ml/12 fl oz double cream

1 tbsp icing sugar

Method

1. Put the pears in a large saucepan with the Marsala, water, brown sugar and lemon rind and gently bring to the boil, stirring to make sure that the sugar has dissolved. Reduce the heat, cover and simmer for 30 minutes until the pears are tender. Leave the pears to cool in the liquid, then remove from the liquid, cover and chill in the refrigerator.
2. Discard the lemon rind and simmer the liquid for 15–20 minutes, or until syrupy. Leave to cool.
3. Cut a thin sliver of flesh from the base of each pear so that they will stand upright. Slit open the vanilla pod and scrape out the seeds into a bowl. Whisk together the cream, vanilla seeds and icing sugar in a bowl until thick. Put each pear on a dessert plate and pour over a little syrup. Serve with the vanilla cream.

ROAST PLUMS WITH ARMAGNAC FOOL

Serves: 6 **Prep: 30 mins** **Cook: 20–25 mins**

Ingredients

- 10 g/¼ oz unsalted butter, for greasing
- 24 ripe plums
- 50 g/1¾ oz unsalted butter
- 2 tbsp maple syrup
- 300 ml/10 fl oz double cream
- 2 tbsp icing sugar
- 2 large egg whites
- 2 tbsp Armagnac or brandy
- finely grated rind of 1 lemon
- 1 tsp rosewater (optional)

Method

1. Preheat the oven to 200°C/400°F/Gas Mark 6. Grease a baking dish with butter.
2. Halve and stone the plums. Place them cut-side up in the prepared dish, dot each one with some of the butter and drizzle over the maple syrup. Cover with foil and bake in the preheated oven for 20–25 minutes until tender. Remove from the oven and leave to cool.
3. Whip the cream in a bowl until beginning to thicken, adding the sugar a little at a time. Whisk the egg whites in a clean, grease-free bowl until they hold stiff peaks. Stir the Armagnac into the cream, then fold in the egg whites, followed by half the lemon rind.
4. To serve, divide the plum halves between six serving dishes and drizzle over the rosewater, if using. Spoon the fool on top of the plums, scatter over the remaining lemon rind and serve immediately.

COMPOTE OF DRIED FRUITS

Serves: 4–6 **Prep: 5 mins** **Cook: 20 mins**

Ingredients

- 140 g/5 oz ready-to-eat dried apricots, halved
- 140 g/5 oz ready-to-eat prunes
- 140 g/5 oz ready-to-eat dried apple rings, halved
- 55 g/2 oz dried cranberries
- 500 ml/17 fl oz orange juice
- 2 pieces stem ginger syrup, drained, reserving osp syrup, and chopped

Method

1. Put the apricots, prunes, apple rings and cranberries into a saucepan and pour over the orange juice.
2. Bring to the boil over a medium heat, then stir in the ginger and reserved syrup. Reduce the heat to low, cover and simmer gently for about 15 minutes, until the fruit is soft.
3. Lift out the fruit with a slotted spoon and place in a serving dish. Simmer the juice, uncovered, for 3–4 minutes, until reduced and slightly thickened.
4. Pour the syrup over the fruit and serve warm or cold.

PEACH MELBA MERINGUE

Serves: 8

Prep: 25 mins, plus cooling

Cook: 50 mins

Ingredients

1 tbsp sunflower oil, for brushing

Raspberry coulis

350 g/12 oz fresh raspberries

115 g/4 oz icing sugar

Meringue

2 tsp cornflour

300 g/10½ oz caster sugar

5 large egg whites

1 tsp cider vinegar

Filling

3 peaches, peeled, stoned and chopped

250 g/9 oz fresh raspberries

200 ml/7 fl oz crème fraîche

150 ml/5 fl oz double cream

Method

1. Preheat the oven to 150°C/300°F/Gas Mark 2. Brush a 35 x 25-cm/14 x 10-inch Swiss roll tin with oil and line with greaseproof paper.
2. To make the raspberry coulis, process the raspberries and sugar to a purée. Press through a sieve into a bowl and set aside.
3. To make the meringue, sift the cornflour into a bowl and stir in the sugar. Whisk the egg whites in a clean, grease-free bowl until they hold stiff peaks, then whisk in the vinegar. Gradually whisk in the cornflour and sugar mixture until the meringue is stiff and glossy.
4. Spread the mixture evenly in the prepared tin, leaving a 1-cm/½-inch border. Bake in the centre of the preheated oven for 20 minutes, then reduce the heat to 110°C/225°F/Gas Mark ¼ and cook for a further 25–30 minutes, or until puffed up. Remove from the oven. Leave to cool for 15 minutes. Turn out onto another piece of greaseproof paper and carefully remove the paper backing.
5. To make the filling, place the peaches in a bowl with the raspberries. Add 2 tablespoons of the coulis and mix. In a separate bowl, whisk together the crème fraîche and cream until thick. Spread over the meringue. Scatter the fruit

over the cream, leaving a 3-cm/1¼-inch border at one short edge. Using the paper, lift and roll the meringue, starting at the short edge without the border, ending up seam-side down. Lift the roll onto a plate and serve with the coulis.

SALTED CARAMEL LAVA CAKES

Serves: 4 **Prep: 20 mins** **Cook: 25 mins**

Ingredients

- 10 g/¼ oz butter, for greasing
- 240 g/8¾ oz plain chocolate, chopped into chunks
- 100 g/3½ oz butter
- 2 eggs
- 2 egg yolks
- 110 g/3¾ oz caster sugar
- 35 g/1¼ oz plain flour
- 1 tsp sea salt flakes
- 4 tbsp dulce de leche (caramel sauce)
- 10 g/¼ oz cocoa powder, for dusting

Method

1. Preheat the oven to 200°C/400°F/Gas Mark 6. Grease four 200-ml/7-fl oz dariole moulds. Place 200 g/7 oz of the chocolate in a small saucepan with the butter and heat over a low heat until smooth and combined.
2. Place the eggs, egg yolks and sugar in a large bowl and beat together until well combined. Pour over the melted chocolate mixture, stir to combine, then fold in the flour.
3. Half fill each of the prepared moulds with the chocolate mixture. Mix the salt into the dulce de leche and place 1 tablespoon of the mixture in the centre of each mould. Top each with a piece of the remaining chocolate. Fill the moulds with the remaining chocolate mixture to 5 mm/¼ inch from the tops of the moulds.
4. Place on a baking tray and bake in the preheated oven for 16 minutes. The cakes should spring back when pressed gently. Carefully turn out the cakes and dust with the cocoa powder. Serve immediately.

CRANBERRY AMARETTI CREAMS

Serves: 10

Prep: 15 mins,
plus cooling & chilling

Cook: 10 mins

Ingredients

85 g/3 oz granulated sugar

2 tsp cornflour

large pinch of ground cinnamon

large pinch of ground ginger

125 ml/4 fl oz water

200 g/7 oz frozen cranberries

150 g/5½ oz full-fat soft cheese

3 tbsp caster sugar

200 ml/7 fl oz double cream

4 tsp orange juice

55 g/2 oz amaretti biscuits, crushed

Method

1 Put the granulated sugar, cornflour, cinnamon and ginger into a heavy-based saucepan, the gradually add the water, stirring, until smooth. Add the cranberries and cook for 5–8 minutes, stirring occasionally, until they are soft and the mixture has thickened. Cover and leave to coc

2 Put the cheese and caster sugar into a mixing bowl and stir, then gradually whisk in the crear until smooth. Stir in the orange juice and then the biscuit crumbs. Spoon the mixture into a disposable paper or polythene piping bag. Spoon the cranberry mixture into a separate disposable piping bag. Snip off the tips.

3 Pipe the amaretti cream into ten shot glasses until they are one-quarter full. Pipe over half th cranberry mixture, then repeat the layers. Cove and chill.

HOLIDAY EGGNOG

Serves: 9

Prep: 10 mins, plus chilling

Cook: 25 mins

Ingredients

- 6 large eggs
- 100 g/3½ oz caster sugar, plus 2 tbsp extra
- 575 ml/18 fl oz single cream
- 575 ml/18 fl oz milk
- 125 ml/4 fl oz brandy
- 4 tbsp light rum
- 1 tsp vanilla extract
- 575 ml/18 fl oz double cream
- freshly grated nutmeg, to decorate

Method

1. Whisk the eggs with a hand-held electric mixer on medium speed until thick and lemon coloured, then gradually add the 100 g/3½ o sugar, whisking well.
2. Put the single cream and milk into a large saucepan over a medium-low heat and heat until very hot but not boiling. Gradually add the hot milk mixture to the egg mixture, stirring with a balloon whisk. Return the mixture to the pan and cook over a medium-low heat, stirrin constantly with a balloon whisk until very hot not boiling. Remove from the heat and leave to cool. Whisk in the brandy, rum and vanilla extract. Cover and chill in the refrigerator.
3. Just before serving, whip the double cream w the remaining sugar in a large bowl until it ho soft peaks. Pour the chilled eggnog mixture in a large punch bowl. Gently fold the whipped cream into the eggnog mixture until just combined. Decorate with freshly grated nutm

MULLED ALE & MULLED WINE

Makes: 2.8 litres/ 5 pints of each | **Prep: 20 mins** | **Cook: 35 mins,** plus standing

Ingredients

Mulled ale

- 2.5 litres/4½ pints strong ale
- 300 ml/10 fl oz brandy
- 2 tbsp caster sugar
- large pinch of ground cloves
- large pinch of ground ginger

Mulled wine

- 5 oranges
- 50 cloves
- thinly pared rind and juice of 4 lemons
- 900 ml/1½ pints water
- 115 g/4 oz caster sugar
- 2 cinnamon sticks
- 2 litres/3½ pints red wine
- 150 ml/5 fl oz brandy

Method

1. To make the mulled ale, put all the ingredients in a heavy-based saucepan and heat gently, stirring, until the sugar has dissolved. Continue heat until simmering, but do not allow it to boi Remove the saucepan from the heat and ser the ale immediately in heatproof glasses.
2. To make the mulled wine, prick the skins of 3 c the oranges all over with a fork and stud with cloves, then set aside. Thinly pare the rind and squeeze the juice from the remaining oranges
3. Put the orange rind and juice, lemon rind and juice, water, sugar and cinnamon in a heavy-based saucepan and bring to the boil over a medium heat, stirring occasionally, until the sugar has dissolved. Boil for 2 minutes without stirring, then remove from the heat, stir once a leave to stand for 10 minutes. Strain the liquid into a heatproof jug.
4. Pour the wine into a separate saucepan and add the strained spiced juices, the brandy and the clove-studded oranges. Simmer gent without boiling, then remove from the heat. Strain the mulled wine into heatproof glasses and serve immediately.

HOT BRANDY CHOCOLATE

Serves: 4

Prep: 5 mins

Cook: 20 mins

Ingredients

- 1 litre/1¾ pints milk
- 115 g/4 oz plain chocolate, broken into pieces
- 2 tbsp sugar
- 4 measures brandy
- 6 tbsp whipped cream
- freshly grated nutmeg, for sprinkling

Method

1. Heat the milk in a small saucepan to just belc boiling point.
2. Add the chocolate and sugar and stir over a low heat until the chocolate has melted.
3. Pour into four warmed heatproof glasses, ther carefully pour 1 measure of the brandy over t back of a spoon into each glass.
4. Add the whipped cream and sprinkle over th grated nutmeg. Serve immediately.

2
3

ELDERFLOWER CHAMPAGNE FIZZ

Serves: 1

Prep: 15 mins, plus infusing

Cook: 15 mins

Ingredients

- 1.5 kg/3 lb 5 oz caster sugar
- 1 litre/1¾ pints water
- 1 lemon, sliced
- 15 elderflower heads, washed
- 40 g/1½ oz citric acid, available from chemists or hardware stores
- ½ measure vodka
- 150 ml/5 fl oz chilled champagne

Method

1. This cocktail takes 24 hours to infuse. In a medium saucepan, bring the sugar and water to a gentle simmer. Turn off the heat and add the lemon slices, elderflower heads and citric acid. Cover the pan and leave to infuse for 24 hours.
2. Strain the syrup through a sieve. Strain again through muslin to catch all the small bits.
3. Pour into sterilized, sealable jars. This syrup will keep for several months in a cool place.
4. Pour ½ measure of the elderflower syrup into a champagne flute. Add the vodka and then top up with the champagne.
5. Serve immediately.

BUCK'S FIZZ

Serves: 1 **Prep: 2 mins** **Cook: No cooking**

Ingredients

2 measures chilled fresh orange juice

2 measures champagne, chilled

Method

1. Half fill a chilled flute with orange juice.
2. Gently pour in the chilled champagne.
3. Serve immediately.

KIR ROYALE

erves: 1 **Prep: 2 mins** **Cook: No cooking**

Ingredients

- drops crème de cassis, or to taste
- ½ measure brandy
- champagne, chilled
- fresh mint spring, to decorate

Method

1. Put the cassis into the bottom of a champagne flute.
2. Add the brandy. Top up with champagne.
3. Decorate with the mint sprig and serve immediately.

AMARETTO, CREAM & BOURBON LAYERS

Serves: 1 **Prep: 2 mins** **Cook: No cooking**

Ingredients

½ measure amaretto

½ measure Irish cream liqueur

½ measure bourbon

Method

1. Gently pour the amaretto into a glass.
2. With a steady hand, carefully pour in the Irish cream liqueur over the back of a teaspoon or bar spoon to make a second layer.
3. Carefully pour in the bourbon in the same way to create a third top layer.
4. Serve immediately.

BEER & RUM FLIP

Serves: 4 **Prep: 5 mins** **Cook: 10 mins**

Ingredients

300 ml/10 fl oz stout
2 measures dark rum
2 measures maple syrup
2 eggs
½ tsp freshly grated nutmeg, to decorate

Method

1. Gently heat the stout in a medium saucepan over a medium heat.
2. Pour the rum and maple syrup into a blender. Crack in the eggs.
3. When the stout has almost come to the boil, pour it carefully into the blender and blend for 30 seconds, or until the contents are nice and frothy.
4. Divide the flip between four snifter glasses and decorate each drink with a little nutmeg.
5. Serve immediately.

PLUM & GINGER WHISKY FIZZ

Serves: 1

Prep: 15 mins, plus infusing

Cook: 15 mins

Ingredients

- 6 ripe plums, stoned and roughly chopped
- large piece of fresh ginger, peeled and sliced
- 2 tbsp granulated sugar
- 3 whole cloves
- 350 ml/12 fl oz whisky
- whole ice cubes
- 1 measure lemon juice
- 175 ml/6 fl oz soda water
- lemon slice, to decorate

Method

1. This cocktail takes 1 week to infuse. Place the plums, ginger, sugar and cloves in a saucepan. Place over a low heat and cook for 5 minutes. Leave to cool. Place the mixture into a sterilized, sealable jar. Add the whisky and mix. Keep the whisky bottle for later use. Seal the jar and leave in a cool place for 1 week to infuse.

2. After 1 week, pour the whisky through a fine sieve and then strain through a coffee filter. Once strained, pour the whisky back into its bottle. Place 2 measures of the whisky in an ice filled cocktail shaker. The remaining whisky can be stored for up to 2 months. Add the lemon juice to the cocktail shaker. Shake vigorously until well frosted, then pour into an ice-filled highball glass. Top up with soda water, decorate with a lemon slice and serve immediately.

BEETROOT VIRGIN MARY

Serves: 1 **Prep: 5–10 mins** **Cook: No cooking**

Ingredients

30 g/1 oz raw beetroot, peeled
175 ml/6 fl oz tomato juice
1 tsp Worcestershire sauce
¼ tsp celery salt
¼ tsp pepper
1 tsp freshly grated horseradish
½ tsp hot pepper sauce
whole ice cubes
1 lemon slice, to decorate
celery stick, to decorate

Method

1. Cut the beetroot into small pieces. Place in a cocktail shaker and crush thoroughly with a muddler or pestle to release the colour and flavour.
2. Add the tomato juice, Worcestershire sauce, celery salt, pepper, horseradish and hot pepper sauce. Stir well with a bar spoon.
3. Pour the mixture into a Collins or highball glass.
4. Add some ice cubes and stir again.
5. Decorate the drink with the lemon slice and celery stick. Serve immediately.

★ Variation

If you're feeling adventurous, try swapping the tomato juice for clamato juice and add your favourite fiery hot sauce!

BAKING & TREATS

GINGERBREAD STAR MUG TOPPERS

Makes: 50

Prep: 25 mins, plus cooling

Cook: 8–10 mins

Ingredients

350 g/12 oz plain flour
175 g/6 oz soft light brown sugar
2 tbsp ground ginger
1 tsp bicarbonate of soda
¼ tsp ground nutmeg
¼ tsp ground mixed spice
115 g/4 oz butter, diced
1 large egg, beaten
100 g/3½ oz golden syrup
2 tbsp plain flour, for dusting
30 g/1 oz icing sugar

Method

1 Preheat the oven to 190°C/375°F/Gas Mark 5. Line two baking sheets with greaseproof pape

2 Put the flour, sugar, ginger, bicarbonate of sodc nutmeg and mixed spice in a food processor and process until the spices are evenly distributed.

3 Add the butter and pulse until fine crumbs forn Add the egg and golden syrup and pulse unti the dough starts to come together.

4 Turn out the dough onto a floured work surface and knead until smooth. Halve the dough and shape into balls.

5 Roll out the dough on a lightly floured surface a thickness of 5 mm/¼ inch. Using a 5.5-cm/2 inch star-shaped cutter stamp out 25 cookies, re-rolling the trimmings as necessary. Place on the prepared baking sheets. Repeat with the remaining dough.

6 Bake the cookies in the preheated oven for 8–10 minutes until the edges are firm. While the cookies are still soft, use a small knife to cut a notch between two points of each star. The notches should be 3–5 mm/⅛–¼-inch wide, depending on the thickness of the mugs you be using.

Transfer to wire racks and leave to cool completely. Dust the cookies with icing sugar and serve.

Variation

For a different topping, sift 250 g/9 oz icing sugar into a bowl and mix with 2 tablespoons of milk to make a smooth icing. Colour with food colouring and use a small knife to spread over the cookies.

RED VELVET SNOWFLAKE COOKIES

Makes: 55

Prep: 45 mins, plus cooling

Cook: 10–14 mins

Ingredients

225 g/8 oz butter, diced and at room temperature

200 g/7 oz caster sugar

1 egg, beaten

1 tbsp red food colouring

1 tsp vanilla extract

1 tsp almond extract

350 g/12 oz plain flour

55 g/2 oz plain flour, for dusting

pinch of salt

Icing

175 g/6 oz icing sugar

5 tsp milk, plus extra as needed

Method

1 Preheat the oven to 180°C/350°F/Gas Mark 4.

2 Line two baking sheets with silicone mats or greaseproof paper, then set aside.

3 Beat the butter and sugar together in a large mixing bowl with an electric mixer until creamy. Beat in the egg, food colouring, vanilla extract and almond extract, beating until the colour is evenly distributed.

4 Sift the flour and salt into the bowl and beat them in. Use your hands to mix the dough into soft ball. Cut the ball into two equal pieces.

5 Roll out one piece of the dough at a time, usin a lightly floured roller on a lightly floured surfac to a thickness of 3 mm/⅛ inch. Use a lightly floured 7.5-cm/3-inch snowflake-shaped cutte to cut out as many cookies as you can, re-rollir the trimmings. Repeat with the remaining doug You should get a total of 55 cookies.

6 Place the cookies on the baking sheets and bake in the preheated oven, in batches, if necessary, for 10–14 minutes until the edges st to brown. Transfer the cookies to wire racks anc leave to cool completely.

7 Meanwhile, make the icing. Sift the icing sugar into a bowl and make a well in the centre. Adc

the milk to the well, stirring in the sugar from the side to avoid lumps. Slowly add more milk, ¼ teaspoon at a time, until the icing is smooth and has a piping consistency. If not using immediately, press a sheet of clingfilm over the surface of the icing to prevent a skin forming.

Spoon the icing into a piping bag fitted with a small plain tip. Carefully pipe pretty decorations onto the cookies. Leave to set for 1 hour, then store in an airtight container, layered with greaseproof paper, for up to 3 days.

CHRISTMAS TREE BISCUITS

Makes: 12

Prep: 15–20 mins, plus chilling

Cook: 10–12 mins

Ingredients

150 g/5½ oz plain flour

1 tsp ground cinnamon

½ tsp freshly grated nutmeg

½ tsp ground ginger

70 g/2½ oz unsalted butter

3 tbsp honey

10 g/¼ oz unsalted butter, for greasing

10 g/¼ oz plain flour, for dusting

narrow ribbon, to decorate

Method

1 Sift the flour, cinnamon, nutmeg and ginger int a bowl and rub in the butter until the mixture resembles breadcrumbs. Add the honey and mix to a soft dough. Halve the dough, shape in balls, wrap in clingfilm and chill in the refrigerat for 30 minutes.

2 Preheat the oven to 180°C/350°F/Gas Mark 4 and lightly grease two baking sheets with butte Roll out one piece of dough on a floured work surface to a thickness of about 5 mm/¼ inch. Cut out tree shapes using a cutter or cardboar template. Repeat with the remaining dough.

3 Put the biscuits on the prepared baking sheets and, using a cocktail stick, make a hole throug the top of each biscuit large enough to thread the ribbon through. Chill the biscuits in the refrigerator for 15 minutes.

4 Bake in the preheated oven for 10–12 minutes until golden. Leave to cool on the baking shee for 5 minutes, then transfer to a wire rack and leave to cool completely. Thread the ribbon through the holes in the biscuits and hang the on the Christmas tree.

CRANBERRY & PINE NUT BISCOTTI

Makes: 18–20 **Prep: 15–20 mins** **Cook: 30–35 mins**

Ingredients

- 10 g/¼ oz butter, for greasing
- 85 g/3 oz light muscovado sugar
- 1 large egg
- 140 g/5 oz plain flour
- ½ tsp baking powder
- 1 tsp ground mixed spice
- 55 g/2 oz dried cranberries
- 55 g/2 oz pine nuts, toasted
- 10 g/¼ oz plain flour, for dusting

Method

1. Preheat the oven to 180°C/350°F/Gas Mark 4. Grease a large baking tray and line it with baking paper.
2. Whisk together the sugar and egg in a large bowl until pale and thick enough to form a trail when the whisk is lifted.
3. Sift together the flour, baking powder and mixed spice into the bowl and fold into the mixture.
4. Stir in the cranberries and pine nuts and lightly mix to a smooth dough.
5. With lightly floured hands, shape the mixture into a long sausage, about 28 cm/11 inches long. Press to flatten slightly.
6. Lift the dough onto the baking tray and bake in the preheated oven for 20–25 minutes, until golden. (Do not switch off the oven.)
7. Leave to cool for 3–4 minutes, then transfer to a board and cut into 1.5-cm/⅝-inch slices. Return the slices to the baking tray.
8. Return to the oven and bake for 10 minutes, or until golden. Remove from the oven, transfer to wire rack and leave to cool completely.

5
7

PAIN AU CHOCOLAT CINNAMON ROLLS

Makes: 12

Prep: 20 mins, plus cooling & standing

Cook: 25–30 mins

Ingredients

- 100 g/3½ oz plain chocolate, broken into pieces
- 320 g/11 oz ready-rolled puff pastry
- 30 g/1 oz unsalted butter, melted
- 2 tbsp caster sugar
- 1½ tsp ground cinnamon

Method

1. Put the chocolate into a heatproof bowl set ove a saucepan of gently simmering water and heat until melted. Remove from the heat, stir un smooth, then leave to cool for 15 minutes, stirrin occasionally.
2. Unroll the pastry and place on a board. Generously brush the pastry with some of the melted butter. Leave to stand for 10 minutes, then spread the cooled chocolate all over the pastry. Mix the sugar and cinnamon together ir a bowl, then sprinkle over the chocolate.
3. Roll up the pastry, Swiss roll-style, from one long side, then brush all over with more of the melte butter. Chill in the refrigerator for 15 minutes. Preheat the oven to 220°C/425°F/Gas Mark 7. Use the remaining melted butter to grease a 12-hole cupcake tin.
4. Using a serrated knife, slice the pastry roll into 1 even-sized rounds. Place each round, cut-side up, in a hole in the prepared tin.
5. Bake in the preheated oven for 15–20 minutes, or until risen and golden brown. Leave to cool i the tin for 5 minutes, then transfer to a wire rack Serve warm or cold.

FESTIVE CUPCAKES

Makes: 14

Prep: 20 mins, plus soaking

Cook: 15–20 mins, plus cooling

Ingredients

- 115 g/4 oz mixed dried fruit
- 1 tsp finely grated orange rind
- 2 tbsp brandy or orange juice
- 85 g/3 oz butter, softened
- 85 g/3 oz soft light brown sugar
- 1 large egg, lightly beaten
- 115 g/4 oz self-raising flour
- 1 tsp mixed spice
- 1 tbsp silver dragées, to decorate

Icing

- 85 g/3 oz icing sugar
- 2 tbsp orange juice

Method

1. Put the dried fruit, orange rind and brandy in a small bowl. Cover and leave to soak for 1 hour.
2. Preheat the oven to 190°C/375°F/Gas Mark 5. Put 14 paper baking cases in 2 cupcake tins or place 14 double-layer paper cases on a baking tray.
3. Put the butter and sugar in a mixing bowl and beat together until light and fluffy. Gradually beat in the egg. Sift in the flour and mixed spice and fold them in with a metal spoon, followed by the soaked fruit. Spoon the mixture into the paper cases.
4. Bake the cupcakes in the preheated oven for 15–20 minutes or until golden brown and firm to the touch. Transfer to a wire rack and leave to cool completely.
5. To make the icing, sift the sugar into a bowl and gradually mix in the orange juice until the mixture is smooth and thick enough to coat the back of a wooden spoon. Using a teaspoon, drizzle the icing in a zig-zag pattern over the cupcakes. Decorate with the silver dragées. Leave to set.

HOLLY CUPCAKES

Makes: 16

Prep: 45 mins, plus cooling

Cook: 20 mins

Ingredients

- 125 g/4½ oz butter, softened
- 200 g/7 oz caster sugar
- 4 eggs, lightly beaten
- a few drops of almond extract
- 150 g/5½ oz self-raising flour
- g/6 oz ground almonds
- 50 g/1 lb white ready-to-roll fondant icing
- 10 g/¼ oz icing sugar, for dusting
- 5 g/2 oz green ready-to-roll fondant icing
-) g/1 oz red ready-to-roll fondant icing

Method

1. Preheat the oven to 180°C/350°F/Gas Mark 4. Line two 8-hole muffin tins with paper cases.
2. Put the butter and caster sugar into a large bowl and beat together until light and fluffy. Gradually beat in the eggs and almond extract. Sift in the flour and, using a metal spoon, fold into the mixture with the ground almonds.
3. Spoon the mixture into the paper cases. Bake the cupcakes in the preheated oven for 20 minutes, or until the cupcakes are risen, golden and firm to the touch. Transfer to a wire rack and leave to cool completely.
4. Roll out the white fondant icing to a thickness of 5 mm/¼ inch on a surface lightly dusted with icing sugar. Using a 7-cm/2¾-inch plain cutter, stamp out 16 rounds, re-rolling the icing as necessary. Place a round on top of each cupcake.
5. Roll out the green fondant icing to the same thickness. Using a holly cutter, cut out 32 leaves, re-rolling the icing as necessary. Brush each leaf with a little water and place two leaves on top of each cupcake. Roll the red fondant icing to make 48 small berries and place on the leaves.

DARK CHOCOLATE YULE LOG

Serves: 8 **Prep: 45 mins,** **plus cooling** **Cook: 20 mins**

Ingredients

10 g/¼ oz butter, for greasing

10 g/¼ oz flour, for dusting

10 g/¼ oz caster sugar, for sprinkling

150 g/5½ oz caster sugar

4 eggs, separated

1 tsp almond extract

115 g/4 oz self-raising flour

280 g/10 oz plain chocolate, broken into squares

225 ml/8 fl oz double cream

2 tbsp rum

holly sprig, to decorate

10 g/¼ oz icing sugar, for dusting

Method

1. Preheat the oven to 190°C/375°F/Gas Mark 5. Grease a 40 x 28-cm/16 x 11-inch Swiss roll tin, line with baking paper, then dust with flour. Sprinkle a sheet of greaseproof paper with caster sugar.
2. Reserving 2 tablespoons, put the caster sugar into a bowl with the egg yolks and whisk until thick and pale. Stir in the almond extract.
3. Whisk the egg whites in a separate bowl until they hold soft peaks. Gradually whisk in the reserved sugar until the mixture is stiff and gloss
4. Sift half the flour into the egg yolk mixture and fold in, then fold in one quarter of the egg white Sift in the remaining flour and fold in, followed b the remaining egg whites.
5. Spoon the mixture into the prepared tin, spreading it evenly with a palette knife. Bake in the preheated oven for 15 minutes, until light golden. Turn out onto the greaseproof paper, then remove the lining paper from the cake if sticking to it, roll up the cake and leave to cool.
6. Place the chocolate in a heatproof bowl. Bring the cream to boiling point in a small saucepan then pour it over the chocolate and stir until the chocolate has melted.

Beat until smooth and thick. Reserve about one third of the chocolate mixture and stir the rum into the remainder. Unroll the cake and spread with the chocolate and rum mixture. Re-roll and place on a large serving plate or silver board.

Evenly spread the reserved chocolate mixture over the top and side of the cake. Mark with a fork so that the surface resembles tree bark. Just before serving, decorate with a holly sprig and sprinkle with icing sugar to resemble snow.

GOLDEN CHRISTMAS CAKE

Serves: 16–18

Prep: 45 mins, plus soaking & cooling

Cook: 1½–2 hours

Ingredients

- 175 g/6 oz dried apricots, chopped
- 85 g/3 oz dried mango, chopped
- 85 g/3 oz dried pineapple, chopped
- 175 g/6 oz sultanas
- 55 g/2 oz chopped stem ginger
- 55 g/2 oz chopped mixed peel
- finely grated rind and juice of 1 orange
- 4 tbsp brandy
- 10 g/¼ oz butter, for greasing
- 175 g/6 oz butter
- 100 g/3½ oz light muscovado sugar
- 4 eggs, beaten
- 2 tbsp clear honey
- 175 g/6 oz self-raising flour
- 2 tsp ground allspice
- 85 g/3 oz pecan nuts, chopped
- 800 g/1 lb 12 oz marzipan
- 900 g/2 lb white ready-to-roll fondant icing
- silver dragées, to decorate

Method

1. Place the apricots, mango and pineapple in a bowl with the sultanas, ginger and mixed peel. Stir in the orange rind and juice and brandy. Cover and leave to soak overnight.
2. Preheat the oven to 160°C/325°F/Gas Mark 3. Grease a 23-cm/9-inch round springform cake tin and line with baking paper.
3. Cream together the butter and sugar until the mixture is pale and fluffy. Add the eggs to the mixture, beating well between each addition. Stir in the honey. Sift the flour with the allspice and fold into the mixture using a metal spoon. Add the soaked fruit and the nuts, mixing thoroughly. Spoon the mixture into the prepared tin, spreading evenly, then make a slight dip in the centre.
4. Bake in the centre of the preheated oven for 1½–2 hours, or until golden brown and firm to the touch and a skewer inserted into the centre of the cake comes out clean. Leave to cool.
5. Unclip and remove the springform, remove the paper and wrap the cake in clean baking paper and foil. Store in a cool place for at least 1 month before using. Cover the cake with marzipan and white fondant icing, then decorate with icing stars and silver dragées.

STOLLEN

Serves: 8

Prep: 1 hour,
plus soaking & rising

Cook: 1 hour

Ingredients

- 50 g/1¾ oz blanched almonds, roughly chopped
- 300 g/10½ oz raisins
- 100 g/3½ oz mixed peel
- 4 tbsp dark rum
- 400 g/14 oz strong white flour, plus extra for dusting
- 250 ml/8½ fl oz lukewarm milk
- 40 g/1½ oz fresh yeast (available in bakeries or online), crumbled
- 3 tbsp clear honey
- 400 g/14 oz softened butter, diced, plus 100 g/3½ oz butter, melted
- 1 tsp salt
- 100 g/3½ oz marzipan, grated
- 2 tsp vanilla extract
- grated zest of 1 lemon
- 150 g/5½ oz icing sugar, plus extra for dusting

Method

1. Pour boiling water over the almonds and leave to soak for 10 minutes. Mix the raisins and mixed peel with the rum.
2. Drain the almonds and mix with the rum and fruit mixture. Leave to soften overnight.
3. Mix together 200 g/7 oz of the flour with the milk, yeast and honey, knead to a dough, then dust with 1 tablespoon of the remaining flour. Leave to rise in a warm place for 30 minutes or until the surface of the dough splits.
4. Mix the remaining flour with the butter, salt, marzipan, vanilla extract, lemon zest and rum-soaked fruit and nuts, then add the dough and knead for 8 minutes.
5. Cover the dough and leave to rise in a warm place for about 1 hour until doubled in size.
6. Meanwhile, preheat the oven to 200 °C/400 °F/ Gas Mark 6. Dust a baking tray with flour. Turn out the dough onto a floured work surface, knead well and place on the prepared baking tray.
7. Bake in the middle of the preheated oven for about 1 hour, covering with baking paper or foil for the last 20 minutes of cooking if it is browning too quickly.

Remove from the oven and brush with the melted butter. Dust with icing sugar, wrap in foil and store in a cool place for about 2 weeks before using. Dredge with the icing sugar just before serving.

TUSCAN CHRISTMAS CAKE

Serves: 14 **Prep: 50 mins** **Cook: 1½ hours**

Ingredients

115 g/4 oz hazelnuts
115 g/4 oz almonds
85 g/3 oz chopped mixed peel
55 g/2 oz ready-to-eat dried apricots, finely chopped
55 g/2 oz candied pineapple, finely chopped
grated rind of 1 orange
55 g/2 oz plain flour
2 tbsp cocoa powder
1 tsp ground cinnamon
¼ tsp ground coriander
¼ tsp freshly grated nutmeg
¼ tsp ground cloves
115 g/4 oz caster sugar
175 g/6 oz clear honey

Method

1. Preheat the oven to 180°C/350°F/Gas Mark 4. Line a 20-cm/8-inch round loose-based cake tin with greaseproof paper.
2. Spread out the hazelnuts on a baking sheet and toast in the preheated oven for 10 minutes until golden brown. Tip them onto a tea towel and rub off the skins. Spread out the almonds on a baking sheet and toast in the oven for 10 minutes until golden
3. Reduce the oven temperature to 150°C/300°F/Gas Mark 2. Chop all the nuts and place in a large bowl. Add the mixed peel, apricots, pineapple and orange rind to the nuts and mix well. Sift in the flour, cocoa powder, cinnamon, coriander, nutmeg and cloves and mix well.
4. Put the sugar and honey into a saucepan and set over a low heat, stirring, until the sugar has dissolved. Bring to the boil and cook for 5 minutes, until thickened and beginning to darken. Stir the nut mixture into the pan and remove from the heat.
5. Spoon the mixture into the prepared tin and smooth the surface. Bake in the oven for 1 hour then transfer to a wire rack and leave to cool completely, then carefully remove from the tin and peel off the greaseproof paper.

WHITE CHOCOLATE & BLACKBERRY MUFFINS

Makes: 12 **Prep: 10–15 mins** **Cook: 25–30 mins**

Ingredients

300 g/10½ oz plain flour
1 tsp baking powder
200 g/7 oz caster sugar
100 g/3½ oz unsalted butter
2 eggs
1 tbsp vanilla extract
275 ml/9 fl oz low-fat natural yogurt
200 g/7 oz blackberries
200 g/7 oz white chocolate, chopped into chunks

Method

1 Preheat the oven to 180°C/350°F/Gas Mark 4. Line a 12-hole muffin tin with paper cases.

2 Sift together the flour, baking powder and sugc into a large bowl. In a separate bowl beat together the butter, eggs, vanilla extract and yogurt until combined.

3 Fold the egg mixture into the flour mixture until just combined; do not over-mix. Stir in the blackberries and chocolate.

4 Spoon the mixture evenly into the paper cases and bake in the preheated oven for 25–30 minutes until golden and cooked through. The muffins should bounce back when pressed gently with a finger. Transfer to a wire rack and leave to cool.

CRANBERRY MUFFINS

Makes: 10

Prep: 20 mins, plus cooling

Cook: 20 mins

Ingredients

- ›sp corn oil, for greasing
- 175 g/6 oz white self-raising flour
- 55 g/2 oz wholemeal self-raising flour
- 1 tsp ground cinnamon
- ›sp bicarbonate of soda
- 1 egg
- 70 g/2½ oz fine-cut marmalade
- 150 ml/5 fl oz semi-skimmed milk
- 5 tbsp corn oil
- 15 g/4 oz eating apple, ›eeled, cored and diced
- 115 g/4 oz fresh or frozen cranberries, thawed if frozen
- 1 tbsp rolled oats

Method

1. Preheat the oven to 200°C/400°F/Gas Mark 6. Grease 10 holes in a silicon muffin tin. Sift together the white flour, wholemeal flour, cinnamon and bicarbonate of soda into a large bowl, tipping in any husks that remain in the sieve.
2. Lightly beat the egg with the marmalade in a large jug, then beat in the milk and oil. Make a well in the centre of the dry ingredients and pour in the beaten liquid ingredients. Gently stir until just combined; do not over-mix. Stir in the apple and cranberries.
3. Divide the mixture evenly between the holes in the prepared tin and sprinkle the oats over the tops of the muffins. Bake in the preheated oven for about 20 minutes, or until well risen, golden brown and firm to the touch.
4. Leave the muffins to cool in the tin for 5 minutes, then serve warm or transfer to a wire rack and leave to cool.

FESTIVE MINCE PIES

Makes: 16

Prep: 30 mins, plus cooling

Cook: 15 mins

Ingredients

- 10 g/¼ oz butter, for greasing
- 200 g/7 oz plain flour
- 100 g/3½ oz butter
- 25 g/1 oz icing sugar
- 1 egg yolk
- 2–3 tbsp milk
- 10 g/¼ oz flour, for dusting
- 300 g/10½ oz ready-made mincemeat
- 1 tbsp milk, for glazing
- 10 g/¼ oz icing sugar, for dusting

Method

1. Preheat the oven to 180°C/350°F/Gas Mark 4. Grease a 16-hole tartlet tin with butter. Sift the flour into a bowl. Using your fingertips, rub in the butter until the mixture resembles breadcrumbs. Stir in the sugar and egg yolk. Stir in enough milk to make a soft dough, then turn out onto a lightly floured work surface and lightly knead until smooth.
2. Shape the dough into a ball and roll out to a thickness of 1 cm/½ inch. Use a 7-cm/2¾-inch fluted cutters to cut out 16 rounds and use to line the holes in the prepared tin. Half-fill each pie with mincemeat. Cut out 16 star shapes from the leftover dough, brush with milk and place one on top of each pie.
3. Glaze the surface of the pies with milk and bake in the preheated oven for 15 minutes until the pastry is a pale golden colour. Remove from the oven and leave to cool on a wire rack. Dust with icing sugar just before serving.

CHRISTMAS CRANBERRY & ORANGE PIES

Makes: 12

Prep: 15 mins, plus cooling

Cook: 30 mins

Ingredients

10 g/¼ oz butter, for greasing

175 g/6 oz frozen cranberries

1 tbsp cornflour

3 tbsp freshly squeezed orange juice

2 star anise

55 g/2 oz caster sugar

225 g/8 oz ready-made sweet shortcrust pastry, chilled

10 g/¼ oz plain flour, for dusting

1 tbsp milk, for brushing

10 g/¼ oz caster sugar, for sprinkling

Method

1 Preheat the oven to 180°C/350°F/Gas Mark 4. Lightly grease a 12-hole mini muffin tin. Put the cranberries in a saucepan with the cornflour and orange juice. Add the star anise and cook over a low heat, stirring occasionally, for 5 minutes, or until the cranberries are soft. Add the sugar and cook for a further 5 minutes, then remove from the heat and leave to cool.

2 Thinly roll out the pastry on a lightly floured surface. Using a 6-cm/2½-inch fluted cookie cutter, stamp out 12 rounds and gently press into the prepared tin, reserving the trimmings. Brush the top edges of the pie cases with a little milk. Remove and discard the star anise, then spoon in the filling.

3 Thinly roll out the pastry trimmings. Using a fluted pastry wheel, cut out thin strips of pastry. Arrange these over each pie in a lattice pattern, brush with milk and sprinkle with sugar. Bake in the preheated oven for 20 minutes. Leave to cool in the tin for 10 minutes, then transfer to a wire rack. Serve warm or cold.

MIXED NUTS IN ROSEMARY SALT

Serves: 4 **Prep: 10 mins** **Cook: 5 mins**

Ingredients

1 tbsp olive oil

2 fresh rosemary sprigs, leaves torn from the stems

55 g/2 oz cashew nuts

55 g/2 oz pecan nuts

55 g/2 oz unblanched almonds

55 g/2 oz unblanched hazelnuts

½ tsp sea salt

Method

1 Heat the oil and rosemary in a medium frying pan, then swirl the oil around the pan to infuse with the rosemary. Add the nuts and cook over a medium heat for 2–3 minutes, until lightly toasted.

2 Stir in the salt, then spoon the nuts into a bowl and leave to cool before eating. Any leftover nuts can be stored in the refrigerator in a plastic container or preserving jar for up to 3 days.

★ Variation

Try replacing the rosemary with a little curry powder or a blend of ground turmeric, garam masala, smoked paprika and a pinch of dried chillies.

CHRISTMAS MACAROONS

Makes: 16

Prep: 40 mins

Cook: 15 mins, plus standing

Ingredients

- 75 g/2¾ oz ground almonds
- 115 g/4 oz icing sugar
- 1 tsp ground mixed spice
- 2 large egg whites
- 50 g/1¾ oz golden caster sugar
- ½ tsp freshly grated nutmeg
- 1 tsp gold dragées

Filling

- 55 g/2 oz unsalted butter, softened
- finely grated rind and juice of ½ orange
- 1 tsp ground mixed spice
- 115 g/4 oz icing sugar, sifted
- 30 g/1 oz glacé cherries, finely chopped

Method

1. Put the ground almonds, icing sugar and mixed spice into a food processor and process for 15 seconds. Sift the mixture into a bowl. Line two baking sheets with greaseproof paper.
2. Place the egg whites in a large clean, grease-free bowl and whisk until they hold soft peaks. Gradually whisk in the caster sugar to make a firm, glossy meringue. Using a spatula, fold the almond mixture into the meringue, one third at time. When all the dry ingredients are thorough incorporated, continue to cut and fold the mixture until it forms a shiny batter with a thick, ribbon-like consistency.
3. Pour the mixture into a piping bag fitted with a 1-cm/½-inch plain nozzle. Pipe 32 small rounds onto the prepared baking sheets. Tap the bakin sheets firmly on a work surface to remove any air bubbles. Sprinkle half the macaroons with the grated nutmeg and gold dragées. Leave to stand at room temperature for 30 minutes. Meanwhile, preheat the oven to 160°C/325°F/ Gas Mark 3.
4. Bake in the preheated oven for 10–15 minutes. Leave to cool for 10 minutes, then carefully pee the macaroons off the paper, place on wire racks and leave to cool completely.

5 To make the filling, beat the butter and orange juice and rind in a bowl until fluffy. Gradually beat in the mixed spice and icing sugar until smooth and creamy. Fold in the glacé cherries. Use to sandwich pairs of macaroons together.

WHITE CHOCOLATE & PEPPERMINT MARSHMALLOWS

Makes: 24

Prep: 45 mins, plus setting

Cook: 25 mins

Ingredients

- 1 tbsp sunflower oil, for greasing
- 1 tbsp cornflour
- 1 tbsp icing sugar
- 25 large marshmallows
- 2–4 drops peppermint extract
- 100 g/3½ oz white chocolate, broken into pieces
- 4 small candy canes, roughly crushed

Method

1. Lightly oil two 12-hole silicone cupcake trays an place on two baking sheets. Sift together the cornflour and icing sugar into a bowl. Use a little of this mixture to lightly dust each hole.
2. Put the marshmallows into a large saucepan with a little water and heat over a medium heat, stirring constantly, for 8–10 minutes, or until melted. Stir in the peppermint extract.
3. Meanwhile, put the chocolate into a heatproof bowl set over a saucepan of gently simmering water and heat until melted. Remove from the heat and stir until smooth. Leave to cool for 10 minutes, stirring occasionally.
4. Gently fold three quarters of the melted chocolate into the marshmallow mixture. Spoon the mixture into the prepared trays.
5. Spoon a small swirl of the remaining melted chocolate onto each marshmallow and sprinkl with the crushed candy canes. Lightly dust the tops with a little of the coating mixture. Leave to set, uncovered, in a cool, dry place for 3–4 hour
6. Carefully remove the marshmallows from the trays. Lightly dust the base and sides with the remaining coating mixture. Store in an airtight container for up to 5 days.

PISTACHIO & APRICOT NOUGAT

Makes: 16 pieces | **Prep: 30 mins, plus setting** | **Cook: 15 mins**

Ingredients

edible rice paper
250 g/9 oz caster sugar
125 ml/4 fl oz liquid glucose
85 g/3 oz clear honey
2 tbsp water
pinch of salt
1 egg white
½ tsp vanilla extract
60 g/2¼ oz unsalted butter, diced and softened
50 g/1¾ oz pistachio nuts, roughly chopped
50 g/1¾ oz ready-to-eat dried apricots, finely chopped

Method

1. Line a 17-cm/6½-inch square loose-based cake tin with clingfilm, leaving an overhang. Line the base with a piece of the rice paper.
2. Put the sugar, glucose, honey, water and salt into a heavy-based saucepan. Heat gently until the sugar has dissolved, tilting the pan to mix the ingredients together.
3. Increase the heat, bring the mixture to the boil and boil for 8 minutes, or until the mixture reaches a temperature of 121°C/250°F on a sugar thermometer.
4. Whisk the egg white in a large clean, grease-free bowl until firm. Gradually pour in a quarter of the hot syrup in a thin stream while continuing to whisk the egg white.
5. Continue whisking for 5 minutes, until the mixture is stiff enough to hold its shape on the whisk.
6. Heat the remaining syrup over a low heat for 2 minutes, or until the mixture reaches 143°C/290°F on a sugar thermometer. Gradually pour the syrup over the egg mixture while beating constantly.
7. Add the vanilla extract and butter and beat for a further 5 minutes. Add the pistachio nuts and apricots and stir.

Pour the mixture into the prepared tin and level with a palette knife. Cover with rice paper and chill in the refrigerator for 8–10 hours, or until fairly firm.

Lift the nougat out of the tin and cut into 16 squares. Store in an airtight container in the refrigerator for up to 5 days.

CHOCOLATE 'SALAMI' LOG

Serves: 12

Prep: 10 mins, plus chilling

Cook: 8 mins

Ingredients

- 75 g/2¾ oz blanched hazelnuts
- 40 g/1½ oz flaked almonds
- 100 g/3½ oz dried figs, roughly chopped
- 2 tbsp triple sec
- 200 g/7 oz plain chocolate, broken into pieces
- 75 g/2¾ oz butter
- 100 g/3½ oz soft light brown sugar
- 1 large egg
- 1 large egg yolk
- zest of 1 orange
- 200 g/7 oz amaretti biscuits
- 50 g/1¾ oz white chocolate chips
- 1 tbsp icing sugar, for dusting

Method

1. Put the hazelnuts and almonds in a large, heavy-based frying pan and heat over a high heat, stirring frequently, until golden brown. Leave to cool slightly, then roughly chop.
2. Place the figs and triple sec in a microwave-proof bowl and heat on High for 1 minute, then set aside.
3. Put the chocolate and butter into a heatproof bowl set over a saucepan of gently simmering water and heat until melted.
4. Meanwhile, beat together the sugar, egg, egg yolk and orange zest in a separate bowl until thick and combined. Add to the chocolate mixture and stir for 5 minutes, or until the sugar completely dissolved.
5. Crush the biscuits into smallish chunks and fold through the chocolate mixture with the figs, nuts and chocolate chips until evenly coated. Spoon the mixture onto a piece of greaseproof paper, shaping into a 20-cm/8-inch log. Tightly roll up the log, twisting both ends to secure. Chill in the refrigerator for 4 hours or overnight.
6. Remove from the refrigerator, dust with the icing sugar and serve. Store in the refrigerator.

ESPRESSO TRUFFLES

Makes: 12

Prep: 40 mins, plus setting

Cook: 5–10 mins

Ingredients

- 300 g/10½ oz plain chocolate, roughly chopped
- 2 tbsp double cream
- 1 tbsp strong espresso coffee, cooled
- 2 tbsp coffee liqueur
- 55 g/2 oz unsalted butter, softened and diced
- edible gold leaf, to decorate (optional)

Method

1. Put 100 g/3½ oz of the chocolate and all the cream into a heatproof bowl set over a saucepan of gently simmering water and heat, stirring, until the chocolate is melted.
2. Remove from the heat, add the coffee, liqueur and butter and whisk for 3–4 minutes, or until thickened. Transfer to an airtight container and chill in the refrigerator for 6–8 hours, or until firm.
3. Line a baking tray with non-stick baking paper. Scoop out teaspoons of the mixture and roll them into truffle-sized balls. Place the balls on the prepared tray, cover with clingfilm and freeze for 6–8 hours.
4. Put the remaining chocolate into a heatproof bowl set over a saucepan of gently simmering water and heat until melted. Using two forks, dip each truffle into the chocolate to coat evenly. Return to the prepared tray and chill in the refrigerator for 1–2 hours, or until firm. Top each truffle with edible gold leaf to decorate, if using. Store in an airtight container in the refrigerator for up to 5 days.

PEANUT BRITTLE

Makes: about 500 g/1 lb 2 oz

Prep: 20 mins, plus cooling

Cook: 15 mins

Ingredients

- 1 tbsp vegetable oil, for oiling
- 200 g/7 oz granulated sugar
- 85 g/3 oz soft light brown sugar
- 85 g/3 oz golden syrup
- 25 g/1 oz butter
- 6 tbsp water
- 175 g/6 oz salted peanuts, roughly chopped
- 1 tsp vanilla extract
- ¼ tsp bicarbonate of soda

Method

1. Preheat the oven to 120°C/250°F/Gas Mark ½. Line a 30-cm/12-inch square baking tray with foil and lightly oil the foil. Place in the preheated oven to warm.
2. Meanwhile, put the granulated sugar, brown sugar, golden syrup, butter and water into a heavy-based saucepan. Heat over a low heat, stirring constantly, until the butter has melted and the sugar has completely dissolved.
3. Brush around the inside of the pan above the level of the syrup with a pastry brush dipped in water, then increase the heat and boil rapidly until the syrup reaches 150°C/300°F ('hard crack' stage).
4. Working quickly, remove from the heat and stir in the peanuts, followed by the vanilla extract and bicarbonate of soda. Pour onto the warmed tray, tipping gently to level the surface. Leave for about 30 minutes to cool, then snap into pieces. Store in airtight bags or containers.

TRADITIONAL BRANDY BUTTER

Serves: 6 **Prep: 20 mins** **Cook: No cooking**

Ingredients

115 g/4 oz unsalted butter, at room temperature

55 g/2 oz caster sugar

55 g/2 oz icing sugar, sifted

3 tbsp brandy

Method

1 Cream the butter in a bowl until it is very smooth and soft. Gradually beat in the caster sugar and icing sugar. Add the brandy, a little at a time, beating well after each addition and taking care not to allow the mixture to curdle.

2 Spoon the brandy butter into a serving dish, cover and chill in the refrigerator until firm. Keep chilled until ready to serve.

NUTTY PEPPERMINT BARK

Makes: 25

Prep: 20 mins, plus chilling

Cook: 3–4 mins

Ingredients

200 g/7 oz red-and-white iped peppermint candy anes, broken into pieces

500 g/1 lb 2 oz white chocolate, roughly chopped

100 g/3½ oz chopped mixed nuts

Method

1. Line a 30 x 20-cm/12 x 8-inch baking tin with non-stick baking paper.
2. Put the broken candy canes into a large polythene food bag and seal tightly. Using a rolling pin, bash the bag until the canes are crushed into small pieces.
3. Put the chocolate into a heatproof bowl set over a saucepan of gently simmering water and heat until melted. Remove from the heat and stir in three quarters of the crushed candy canes.
4. Pour the mixture into the prepared tin, smooth the surface using a spatula and sprinkle over the chopped nuts and remaining candy. Press down very slightly to ensure they stick. Cover with clingfilm and chill in the refrigerator for 30 minutes, or until firm.
5. Break the peppermint bark into small, uneven pieces. Store in an airtight container in a cool, dry place for up to 2 weeks.

PISTACHIO & CHERRY CHOCOLATE BISCOTTI

Makes: 40

Prep: 25 mins, plus cooling

Cook: 45 mins

Ingredients

- 2 sprays non-stick cooking spray
- 250 g/9 oz plain flour
- 125 g/4½ oz wholemeal flour
- ¼ tsp salt
- 200 g/7 oz granulated sugar
- 3 eggs
- 2 tbsp vegetable oil
- 1 tbsp vanilla extract
- 40 g/1½ oz dried cherries, roughly chopped
- 60 g/2¼ oz roasted, unsalted pistachio nuts
- 10 g/¼ oz flour, for dusting
- 280 g/10 oz plain chocolate, chopped

Method

1. Preheat the oven to 180°C/350°F/Gas Mark 4 and line a large baking sheet with baking paper. Spray the paper with cooking spray.
2. Put the plain flour, wholemeal flour and salt into a mixing bowl.
3. Put the sugar and eggs into a separate large mixing bowl and beat with a hand-held electric mixer on high speed for 3–4 minutes, or until the mixture is thick and pale yellow. Add the oil and vanilla extract and beat to incorporate. Add the dry mixture to the wet mixture and beat on low speed until just combined. Add the cherries and nuts and mix to incorporate.
4. Divide the dough into two pieces and turn them out onto the prepared baking sheet. With floured hands, shape each piece of dough into a 25-cm/10-inch loaf and flatten it to 2.5 cm/ 1 inch, squaring off the edges with your hands.
5. Bake in the preheated oven for 25 minutes, or until light brown. Remove from the oven and leave to cool on the baking sheet for about 10 minutes. Meanwhile, reduce the oven temperature to 160°C/325°F/Gas Mark 3.
6. Slice each loaf into about 20 x 1-cm/½-inch thick slices. Arrange cut side down on the baking sheet and return to the oven for a further

10 minutes. Flip the slices over and bake for a further 10 minutes. Transfer to a wire rack and leave to cool completely.

7 Put the chocolate into a heatproof bowl set over a saucepan of gently simmering water and heat until melted. Dip one flat side of each of the biscotti into the melted chocolate, then return to the lined baking sheet, uncoated side down, and leave to cool for 10–15 minutes until the chocolate is set. Serve at room temperature.

Makes: 16 pieces

Prep: 15 mins, plus setting

Cook: 10–15 mins

Ingredients

- 1 tbsp sunflower oil, for oiling
- 250 g/9 oz soft brown sugar
- 100 g/3½ oz unsalted butter, diced
- 400 ml/14 fl oz canned sweetened full-fat condensed milk
- 2 tbsp glucose syrup
- 150 g/5½ oz plain chocolate, roughly chopped
- 60 ml/2 fl oz whisky
- 30 g/1 oz walnut pieces

Method

1. Lightly brush a 20-cm/8-inch square baking tin with oil. Line it with non-stick baking paper, snipping diagonally into the corners, then pressing the paper into the tin so that the base and sides are lined.
2. Put the sugar, butter, condensed milk and glucose syrup into a heavy-based saucepan. Heat gently, stirring, until the sugar has dissolved.
3. Increase the heat, bring to the boil and boil for 12–15 minutes, or until the mixture reaches 116°C/240°F on a sugar thermometer (if you don't have a sugar thermometer, spoon a little of the syrup into some iced water; it will form a soft ball when it is ready). As the temperature rises, stir the fudge occasionally so the sugar doesn't stick and burn. Remove the fudge from the heat. Add the chocolate and whisky and stir together until the chocolate has melted and the mixture is smooth.
4. Preheat the grill to medium-hot. Put the walnuts on a baking tray and toast them under the grill for 2–3 minutes, or until brown, then roughly chop them.
5. Pour the mixture into the prepared tin, smooth the surface using a spatula and sprinkle over the walnuts. Leave to cool for 1 hour. Cover with

clingfilm, then chill in the refrigerator for 1–2 hours, or until firm. Lift the fudge out of the tin, peel off the paper and cut into small squares. Store in an airtight container in a cool, dry place for up to 2 weeks.

CHOCOLATE CHUNK STICKS

Makes: 10–15

Prep: 5–10 mins, plus cooling

Cook: 5–10 mins

Ingredients

- 200 g/7 oz plain chocolate, milk chocolate or white chocolate, or a mixture, finely chopped
- 2–4 tbsp instant coffee granules
- 2–4 tbsp desiccated coconut
- 2-4 tbsp toasted nuts
- 2–4 tbsp mini marshmallows
- 2–4 tbsp chocolate vermicelli
- 2-4 tbsp edible glitter
- 1.2 litres/2 pints semi-skimmed milk or full-fat milk, to serve

Method

1. Put the chocolate into a heatproof bowl set ove a saucepan of gently simmering water and hec until melted. If you are using different chocolate melt them in separate bowls.
2. Divide the chocolate between silicone moulds, a silicone ice tray or small paper cases. Leave to cool slightly until the chocolate begins to thicken, then push a small wooden spoon, lollipop stick or wooden coffee stirrer into each mould so it stands upright.
3. While the chocolate is still soft, scatter each stick with a topping of your choice (instant coffee granules, desiccated coconut, toasted nuts, min marshmallows, chocolate vermicelli or edible glitter), then leave to set solid.
4. To serve, heat a mug of milk for each chocolate chunk stick. Remove any paper cases and stir a stick into each mug of hot milk until melted. Serve immediately.

INDEX

This edition published by Parragon Books Ltd in 2016
LOVE FOOD is an imprint of Parragon Books Ltd

Parragon Books Ltd
Chartist House
15–17 Trim Street
Bath BA1 1HA, UK
www.parragon.com/lovefood

ISBN 978-1-4748-3795-8

Printed in China

Introduction by Anne Sheasby
Cover and new photography by Al Richardson
New recipes by Beverly Le Blanc

Notes for the Reader
This book uses both metric and imperial measurements. Follow the same units of measurement throughout; do not mix metric and imperial. All spoon measurements are level: teaspoons are assumed to be 5 ml, and tablespoons are assumed to be 15 ml. Unless otherwise stated, milk is assumed to be full fat, eggs and individual fruits and vegetables are medium, pepper is freshly ground black pepper and salt is table salt. A pinch of salt is calculated as 1/16 of a teaspoon. Unless otherwise stated, all root vegetables should be peeled prior to using.

The times given are an approximate guide only. Preparation times differ according to the techniques used by different people and the cooking times may also vary from those given.

For best results, use a food thermometer when cooking meat. Check the latest government guidelines for current advice. Please consume alcohol responsibly.

150
RECIPES
series
150
BAKING
recipes
150
CAKE
recipes
150
CHICKEN
recipes
150
CHRISTMAS
recipes
150
CUPCAKE
& MUFFIN
recipes
150
FAST
& SIMPLE
recipes
150
GLUTEN-FREE
recipes
150
GRANDMA'S
recipes
150
HEALTHY
recipes
150
INDIAN
recipes
150
ONE-POT
recipes
150
PASTA
recipes
150
SLOW
COOKER
recipes
150
STIR-FRY
recipes
150
STUDENT
recipes
150
TAPAS
recipes
150
VEGETARIAN
recipes